T0015386

"A fantastic and engaging rollercoaster ride through Judy's life, especially as the entrepreneurial and brilliant publisher she became. In these pages lie inspiration, encouragement, overcoming tragic events and, ultimately, well-earned success. A powerful memoir from a woman who stormed into the world of publishing and put her indelible stamp on it."

Malcolm Stern, Psychotherapist, Author and Co-founder of Alternatives

"An inspirational read – especially for aspiring female entrepreneurs. Judy shares her experiences with candour, and her tenacity and persistence lead to a fantastic exit. A must-read."

Charlotte Mason, INSEAD Start-up Bootcamp Director and Venture Partner @ Antler

"An inspiring book, especially for anyone who has dreamed of building a rewarding business, but thought it impossible. Judy Piatkus takes you step by step from her first job as a secretary with poor typing skills to the sale of her enormously successful Piatkus Books, without neglecting the painful and joyful milestones in her personal life. The implicit message is 'if I can do it, so can you!'"

Dr Dina Glouberman, Author, Psychotherapist and Co-Founder of Skyros Holidays

"This book is bursting with entrepreneurial energy, wisdom and life experience. Having been at primary and secondary school through the '80s and '90s when the majority of this book is set, I found it utterly fascinating to read about the intricacies and day-to-day details of doing business at this time. The author also gives great insight into the world of publishing as an added bonus to an already very informative and engaging book. You won't fail to be inspired and uplifted by this book."

Lucy Mullins, Entrepreneurship Expert with the Entrepreneurship Centre at the Saïd Business School, University of Oxford, Co-Founder of StepLadder and Co-Founder of #RideTheWave Professional Coaching.

"If you found yourself talking about mindfulness, reincarnation, astrology or feng shui at a dinner party recently, it was probably because of a Piatkus book (even if you didn't know it). This is Judy's honest, gossipy, fascinating story of how she created a multi-million selling book brand that sent the New Age mainstream. I loved it."

Jessica Adams, Astrologer and Author

"Judy Piatkus truly does have a passion for books, but equally for helping others to achieve their own real potential, allied to a zest for living and overcoming obstacles, that will inspire many women to become the best they can be, in any field. Few women were forging careers when Judy set out on this journey and yet, indomitable in the face of setbacks, and learning as she went along, she succeeded in setting up her own publishing house. In sharing her experiences here, she will enable a whole new generation of female entrepreneurs to follow their dream of setting up a business of their own."

Trisha Ashley, *Sunday Times* Bestselling Author

"Judy is a publishing legend who has written a riveting memoir. Graceful and witty, it opens a fascinating window on the entrepreneurial life. A brilliant read."

Julia Hobsbawm OBE, Entrepreneur and Broadcaster

"Truly amazing story of courage and following your dreams. Extraordinary life, extraordinary women and a wonderful book.

The name Piatkus will always be synonymous with pioneering Mind, Body, Spirit books. I first met Judy, sitting in her office discussing my first book, so to have an opportunity to read this memoir that gives a peek into what it takes to succeed as a woman in publishing is pure gold. This book will inspire and support all those still dreaming of living a meaningful and conscious life. Thank you, Judy."

Caroline Shola Arewa, Coach, Speaker, Trainer, Author of Opening to Spirit and Energy 4 Life

"*Ahead of Her Time* provides amazing insight into the journey and achievements of an extraordinary woman. In this candid, honest and often deeply touching story, Judy Piatkus generously shares the innate wisdom, insights and foresights that enabled her to journey from being a secretary and mother of three with a vision, to becoming a respected and greatly revered world class publisher. This inspirational book is an absolute must-read!"

Maryon Stewart, BEM, Wellbeing Coach, Author and Broadcaster

"I have known Judy for many years and this lovely memoir is the story of her extraordinary life, bringing up her family while, at the same time, growing a market-leading business. It is interesting to discover how the history of publishing in the UK has developed and how she was constantly adapting her business to meet the changing needs of her readers. The book also explores Judy's personal journey of self-discovery. As her readers changed, so did she. Her realism and optimism shine throughout the book and reading it will be an inspiration to anyone juggling business and family life."

Oonagh Harpur, Building trust and integrity in the boardroom

Ahead of her time

Audiobooks by the same author:

Grow Your Business to Survive and Thrive During
Challenging Times
How Trendspotting Can Help Your Business Take Off
How to Grow a Great Business
The Entrepreneurial Experience: Managing Your
Business through Tough Times
How to Find Your Perfect Partner

Writing as Judy Ashberg:

Little Book of Women's Wisdom
Wisdom for Lovers

Ahead of her time

JUDY PIATKUS

How a One-Woman
Startup Became a
Global Publishing Brand

WATKINS
Sharing Wisdom Since 1893

This edition first published in the UK and USA in 2021 by
Watkins, an imprint of Watkins Media Limited
Unit 11, Shepperton House
89-93 Shepperton Road
London
N1 3DF

enquiries@watkinspublishing.com

1 2 3 4 5 6 7 8 9 10

Typeset by Lapiz

Printed and bound in in the UK by TJ Books Ltd

A CIP record for this book is available from the British Library

ISBN: 978-1-78678-531-2 (Hardback)
ISBN: 978-1-78678-567-1 (ebook)

www.watkinspublishing.com

For every woman who has the courage to follow her dreams

CONTENTS

FOREWORD

In 2008, I founded Addidi Wealth to help women create, invest and enjoy their wealth, and in 2009 I launched the Addidi Inspiration Awards. I wanted to celebrate ordinary women, past and present, who – like Judy Piatkus – led amazing lives that we don't always hear about. I wanted to acknowledge women who had created wealth, or who devoted their lives to their professions or community for the greater good, or who had simply made us happy! Judy embodies the spirit of all these: she has created significant wealth, she is generous and she always has a smile on her face.

For me, Judy's book is a hit on so many levels. It's a story I can relate to personally, as someone who founded and sold my own business and also as a woman balancing work, family and me-time. It's the story of an ordinary woman who created an extraordinary life for herself and her family. Like so many women I have had the privilege of working with, Judy had the quiet determination, the focus and the sheer willpower to keep going, day in and day out, as she created a successful business while balancing her family life and work life as best she could.

Through tough times and good times, she kept her head down, stayed focused and didn't compromise on her caring and nurturing self.

More importantly, the book reconfirms my belief that women excel when they have the freedom to live a life, in and out of business, in which they don't have to put limits on who and what they can be. In a world designed primarily by men for men, it's not a road that's easily travelled by women – but Judy did it and this book explains how.

She is a great role model for women with ambition who wish to balance family and business, and her book provides plenty of motivation to keep going when times are tough. We need more women like Judy, and like me, who set up businesses, who don't compromise on their values and who allow themselves the time and focus to make a success of their enterprises. Judy and her book should be up there with the likes of Dame Stephanie Shirley and Anita Roddick, acknowledged and celebrated by all.

Anna Sofat
Voice of Women's Wealth, Founder & CEO Addidi Wealth
and Associate Director, Progeny Wealth

ONE
MY FIRST JOB

Some people come into the world and are recognized from an early age as born entrepreneurs; others are hewn and shaped by the circumstances of their lives. In my case, I started with a strong advantage. From an early age, I was programmed by my parents to have a career. Not just any career, either, but a brilliant and successful one. No one in my family suggested how this might be achieved, as there was nothing for which I showed a particular talent. There was also a very mixed message attached to this powerful parental vision for my life. My brilliant career would need to come to an end on the day I walked down the aisle. My mother had given up her job in order to put her exceptionally good organizational talents to use in the home – and so, it seemed, would I.

My parents, Ralph and Estelle Assersohn, met and married just after the Second World War. Both were in their thirties, and their views about life and child-rearing were somewhat Victorian. My younger sister, Rosalind, and I were brought up to be seen and not heard, and to be "good little girls". My parents always wanted the best for us and I never doubted that they loved and cared for me as much as they were able. However, although I would always think of my childhood as a happy one, it wasn't because I had a close relationship with either of them or with my sister. I often felt like a cuckoo in the nest and that I disappointed my parents by failing to behave in the conventional ways they expected. I was, in their eyes, fairly wilful and in their quest for the "perfect daughter" they didn't know how to respond to the freedom-loving rebel in me, which was a regular cause of disappointment for everyone.

My father, who was employed as the managing director of a small building firm, was definitely not a man suited to entrepreneurship. My mother, intense and highly strung, was typical of the generation that American women's activist Betty Friedan wrote about in *The Feminine Mystique*: dissatisfied housewives frustrated with the limitations of their lives and needing to find personal fulfilment outside the home. My mother was a highly capable woman with a good brain, who would have been a wonderful entrepreneur had she been born in a different era or married to a different man. When I was older, I would think of her as a "professional housewife", as every activity to which she turned her hand was completed in the most accomplished way. I had also recognized that none of it had been sufficient to contain her unconscious frustrations.

This was possibly the main reason I decided that being a stay-at-home wife and mother was not for me. It wasn't destined to be plain sailing from the start, though, and my brilliant career began with a jolt. While I had always been a voracious reader, as a teenager I also spent a good deal of time away from home, socializing with friends in the North West London suburbs where I lived. Partly as a result of my partying, I failed to get the grades I needed for university and was duly sent off to learn shorthand and typing. My mother had always stressed that every woman needed to have some money of her own and I needed to be suitably equipped to earn it.

My first job was working for the production manager at John Murray, a venerated 200-year-old publishing company based in a gracious house in Albemarle Street, on the corner of Piccadilly. I was a fast typist, though not always an accurate one. Luckily, in this job, I was only required to type short notes to the printers, while I endeavoured to get my head around some of the obscure production terminology. Sometimes I was asked to fill in on reception and take the calls on the old-fashioned switchboard, where I would plug in wires to different extensions. "I'm putting you through now," I would say, with the earphones over my head. It was hard to imagine that this would be the start of my brilliant career.

Realizing that book production was not something which interested me, I searched out a different job in publishing. My next position was working as a secretary in the publicity department at Cassell, another venerable English publishing company, founded in 1848. From there, after only a few months, I applied for the post of assistant publicity manager at the company Robert Hale, which looked like a step up. I got the job, which turned out to be great fun. The publicity manager, John Gittens, had been in his role for over twenty years and was happy to sit at his desk and let me do the running around. Robert Hale published a range of non-fiction and very downmarket commercial fiction. My job consisted of basic publicity skills, sending out review copies, arranging interviews and learning to understand budgets and when it would be appropriate to spend money advertising a book.

John also asked me to take literary editors at the major London newspapers out to lunch, where I was to tell them about our new books. He had been doing it for twenty years and thought the middle-aged male editors might pay more attention to a lively young woman. I had a generous expense account, a ready smile and I was always eager to learn more about the world of books and publishing; so it was both a delicious and terrifying surprise to find myself, at the tender age of twenty-one, wining and dining some of the most erudite and knowledgeable people in the literary world. Totally out of my depth, of course, but so young and ignorant that people forgave my lack of knowledge and I was able to secure occasional attention for some of our titles.

It was here, at Robert Hale, that I enjoyed my first taste of entrepreneurship. I asked to become a reader for the company in my spare time and was paid three guineas per book. It was the first time I had had to form my own opinions about commercial fiction, and although my advice was not always taken, it was useful nonetheless – as was the extra income, as I was only earning £20 a week.

After about a year, still concerned at my low salary and continuing lack of status, I felt something needed to be done to further my brilliant career – so, on the side, I started a small literary agency with the managing director John Hale's secretary, Gill Boyd, a competent young woman around my own age. The impetus for this venture had unconsciously come from my parents. At the age of eleven, I had bypassed a year of school when I won a scholarship to a local private school, South Hampstead High, and as a result of that achievement, the concept of the brilliant career I was going to have had been deeply instilled into me. I was later to appreciate that, even at this young age, in my early twenties, and in spite of not having any idea how the commercial world worked, I was already starting to look for "the edge" – the elusive opportunity that was going to lead to the mysterious great achievement that would, hopefully, make my long-suffering parents proud of me at last.

Gill and I agreed verbally to divide any proceeds between us 50/50, but we did not know anything about starting a business and had no idea how little we really did know. As far as I can remember, we did not even know enough to draw up a written agreement between ourselves, let alone make a business plan, define our vision or create our goals. We printed some headed notepaper and opened a bank account together (it was very easy to do that in the 1970s), into which we put a very small amount of money, which we quickly spent on taking out an advertisement in an appropriate publication. Authors began to send us material, and one writer sent us a few short stories which we effortlessly sold to the *Evening News*. We were sent a few novels to read and returned most of them, although there were one or two we liked. We were wondering how to go about submitting them to publishers when I received a letter from an editor at Constable Books, inviting me out for lunch to discuss what we had to offer them.

It was at that point I realized the game was up. I knew I didn't want to go to lunch and have a conversation about what we were doing. As Gill and I weren't really sure ourselves where we intended to go with this particular venture, we decided that we should perhaps give up this particular dream until we had both learned more about the publishing industry. (Strangely, this first entrepreneurial venture did end up making a profit. The local branch of our bank made a mistake and paid us a small sum of money that had not been generated by either of our efforts. In spite of our honesty, they insisted the error was not theirs.)

I decided at this point that I would look for a job in a real literary agency and learn how the agency side of publishing worked. It was 1971 and I was about to get married, something that in no way put me off my career stride. I had met my husband-to-be, Brian Piatkus, some years previously at a party given by a work colleague. He was a few years older than me and a clever man. He was a clinical chemist, working in an NHS hospital and studying part-time for a master's degree. We had little money between us but we seemed to share common values and sparked each other off in a lively way. I bade a fond farewell to my lovely boss and went off to become a literary agent with a salary rise to £25 a week.

Rupert Crew Associates was run by two delightful middle-aged ladies, Doreen Montgomery and Shirley Russell, both very experienced agents who had worked together for many years. They got on well and laughed a lot, and I remember the atmosphere in the office as being rather jolly. Their major clients were Barbara Cartland, the romance writer, and Cecil Beaton, the Oscar-winning stage and costumer-designer who was also a distinguished fashion, portrait and war photographer. It was a small company and I would have a chance to learn everything that was going on. But there was a catch I hadn't foreseen. A lot of my time was spent typing letters and long contracts – but my typing was simply not good enough. In those days of manual typewriters and no correcting ribbons, every mistake was one too many, especially on a contract with its many clauses. After my three-month trial period, I was told that I would have to leave. I hadn't enjoyed all the typing, but I had started to learn about the business of being a literary agent and, with my naturally optimistic nature, had assumed that my skills would improve with all the effort I was putting in. This was not simply a blow to my self-esteem: my husband and I needed my salary to pay the mortgage each month. There was no time to waste. I had to find another job.

David Higham Associates was another old and established literary agency in the London publishing world at that time. It had been founded by David Higham in the 1930s and by the time I became his secretary he was in his late seventies; a tall, commanding presence with a head of white hair and a certain abruptness of manner. He had had so many secretaries in his time that he had long ago stopped worrying about badly typed letters. Whenever I made a mistake, he simply crossed it out and scribbled the correct word over it. He would arrive in the office each morning in a taxi from his home in Keats Grove, Hampstead, and would dictate letters and memos before lunching every day at his own special table at L'Etoile restaurant in Charlotte Street. Sometimes he would invite one of his prestigious authors to lunch with him, such as Eric Hobsbawm, A. J. P. Taylor, James Lees-Milne – the agency client list was a roll call of some of the greatest writers, historians and thinkers of the century. Unexpectedly I had found myself a job at the heart of publishing.

Because David Higham's hours in the office were limited, he couldn't always find enough work for me to do. So when a fairly new company, White Lion, approached the David Higham agency to ask if they could reprint some of the out-of-print books from the sizeable agency backlist (the range of books they had sold to publishers over the years, which they continued to look after for their authors), I asked if I could research which of the older titles might be suitable. Over several months, I scoured the agency's list of living authors and literary estates, and sourced a range of ancient hardback copies, which I offered to White Lion for reprinting. They bought a fair number and suddenly I was earning money for the agency. I was given a rise to £28 a week – for which I hadn't thought to ask – and was told that if I came across a new author who would be a suitable client for the agency, I would be allowed to represent him or her. I was also given some anonymous typescripts to read and comment on, to assess my literary judgement. Very soon, I realized that literary fiction wasn't entirely my thing, as I didn't enjoy some of the novels I was asked to read and was shocked to discover they had been written by very eminent novelists. I began to doubt that being an agent was for me.

I managed to commission one successful book for David Higham, though, before I decided to leave the agency. The author was an agony aunt for a popular newspaper and my mother was a friend of her sister. I wrote to ask if she would like to write a book – she hadn't written one before – and she agreed to become a client of the agency. My legacy to David Higham Associates was a book published in 1975 by Marjorie Proops, doyenne of agony aunts, whose column *Dear Marje* in the *Daily Mirror* had made her a household name.

I never did discover how to become a literary agent because an entrepreneur avenue opened just then, and I seized it. Edwin Buckhalter, with whom I had been dealing at White Lion, and I decided to set up our own company together, a bold and brave venture, but this time I had much more understanding of what was involved.

Suddenly my career was on the up. I was going to be my own boss.

TWO

EDWIN

I was twenty-four and Edwin a year older when we launched Severn House in 1974. Having been programmed by my parents and schooling to have a successful career, I saw the opportunity of starting my own business as a new and exciting step. I didn't have strong feelings about whether I wanted to work for a company or work for myself. Career success for women was not a societal concept at that time. It wasn't essential for either men or women to obtain a degree in order to get an interesting job. Several of my women friends had become teachers or worked in their family businesses before settling down in hopeful married bliss to have children. The boyfriends and soon-to-be husbands in my social circle were becoming doctors, dentists, lawyers and accountants. I had little self-knowledge and did not realize how exceptionally ambitious I was. There were few female role models, although Germaine Greer's bestseller *The Female Eunuch* was opening people's minds to new thinking about women's place in society. The country was seemingly run by middle-aged, upper-class white men. *Cosmopolitan* magazine's careers advice was still just in its infancy, as the UK edition of the magazine had only been launched in 1972. There were no programmes on the television or reading material to inspire me.

My father had talked about the building trade with my mother at home every night, but his conversation was never addressed to me and I do not remember learning anything about business from him. I did not have a vision of what success would look or feel like – except that I would presumably earn more money. Was I looking for my parents to approve of me at last, to fulfil their expectations of the perfect daughter? Would I be taken more seriously by them as a person in my own right? Perhaps – and yet I knew my mother would have preferred me to have had the time to go shopping with her rather than spend all day in an office. Even now I cannot be sure of all the motives that continued to propel me upwards, towards something so much greater than I could even begin to imagine, so limited was my knowledge of the commercial world at that time.

As the son of a London bookseller who supplied libraries, my new business partner, Edwin, had grown up surrounded by books. Our friendship had developed while we had worked closely together in our previous positions, and we shared the same sense of humour. We could chat to one another happily for hours, but in fact both of us were ambitious and seemed to be well matched, happy to take on the joint responsibilities that an enterprise such as the one we envisioned would require. Edwin was naturally good with figures and developed a simple financial plan for our new enterprise, which showed that we would need to raise £5,000 between us. This would be our start-up capital. I had no idea where my half of the money would come from, as I was still employed by the David Higham agency on my meagre salary of £28 per week.

Nevertheless, I had always been a saver since my teenage years. My parents were never mean, but they were always prudent about their purchases and I tended to follow their example, careful in how I spent my money. Indeed, there wasn't a lot that I usually wanted for myself aside from books, many of which I borrowed from the library, and clothes, which I considered a necessity rather than anything I might be tempted to splurge on. I did, though, always try to dress as well as I could afford, as I thought I would be taken more seriously if I looked the part. Occasionally, I still glimpse the friendly yet rather shy young woman I was at that time in the few faded photographs I have kept from those years. I was slim with unruly, wavy dark hair, which still goes frizzy at the slightest hint of rain, and I was usually neatly dressed in skirts and jumpers that I had curated carefully, buying them from Marks & Spencer or John Lewis in Oxford Street in my lunch hour.

Although now a married woman whose income was needed to make a major contribution to the household, I had always remembered my mother's advice to make sure I had some money of my own. Tucked away in a building society account, I had some savings from an unexpected and generous wedding present given to me by my mother's brother, the only entrepreneur in the family, as well as a small amount of money saved from reading for Robert Hale over the years. Nevertheless, I was still a little bit short of covering my share of what was needed.

I hated asking my parents for anything, let alone money. Reluctantly, because I had always been very independent and had been brought up by my father never to borrow anything from anyone, I asked him for a loan of £500. This was a lot of money for him to find – he and my mother had recently paid for my and Brian's wedding and helped us with the deposit on our flat – but he generously wrote me a cheque and I promised to pay him back as soon as I could. Little did I imagine at that time what would eventually become of this starting capital of £2,500, my initial "skin in the game".

We chose the name "Severn House" for the company because Edwin had a passion for music and especially for the music of the composer Edward Elgar. Severn House was the name of Elgar's house in London, chosen for the composer's affinity with the River Severn and the Worcestershire countryside where he grew up. We divided the shares of the new company 50/50, and the plan was that we would publish reprints of several books in hardback each month, which we would sell to the library market. Some of the books were early works by authors who had subsequently become well known and which, because the quality varied, some publishers had been reluctant to reprint, even though there was a market for many authors' earlier works through their growing fanbase. Other books that we chose to publish had been popular in the past but had been out of print for many years, so we approached the authors' literary estates for permission to give these older books a new lease of life.

I was responsible for finding the books. This meant that I would visit publishers and literary agents and search through their backlists for fiction that we thought we would be able to sell in sufficient quantities to turn a profit. I would draw up the contracts – I had learned quite a lot about contracts from working at David Higham Associates (and especially about getting a basic boilerplate template pre-printed so I didn't have to type a new one each time) – and then together we would think about how we might maximize the sales potential of each book, although our opportunities were fairly limited as our contracts to reprint did not give us much scope for finding other ways to profit from our investment.

Edwin was in charge of the book costings and the overall finances. His work also included negotiating with the printers and ensuring that all the titles were produced in time for our scheduled publication dates. Together we would visit our main customers, the large wholesalers who supplied libraries direct. In the 1970s, libraries were well funded and able to buy sizeable quantities of all kinds of books. The number of books being published in the UK was far fewer than now – self-publishing was extremely rare – and libraries were an important part of the culture of the nation.

Severn House was not required to supply individual libraries directly, because each library authority had their own very specific requirements about how they wanted to manage their inventory. Some wanted their books covered in their own carefully chosen, hardwearing bookbinding materials, while others would request a stamp of ownership on a specific page. It was labour-intensive work supplying the different authorities, and the library wholesalers were very good at it.

Most important of all, from the point of view of a start-up enterprise, the library wholesalers ordered well in advance and could pay us on time. As they were our main customers, we would visit them regularly and ask their advice about which authors would be best to publish. The buyers were extremely encouraging and supportive of two young people trying to grow a business. Especially, I imagine, as one of them was a woman; there were so few women in senior positions. No one ever talked about "businesswomen" back then. The library wholesalers' buyers, who decided which titles they were going to take and in what quantity, were very knowledgeable and understood their market, so they were often pleased to know that popular authors would be coming back into print. Their job was to keep their customers happy too.

At first, I worked out of the spare bedroom of the small flat I shared with Brian in East London. Edwin had moved back to live with his parents. We spoke on the phone frequently and met occasionally, usually because we both needed to be at a meeting elsewhere together. For three years it all went brilliantly. Working in harmony, we did what we were both supposed to do very well. We both loved our business, getting up each day to focus on our responsibilities. The fact that we were rarely together meant that when we did see each other, we were very focused on what we needed to achieve.

Gradually the company began to become known. Our consistency in publishing a similar number of titles each month meant that we were taken seriously in our own very tiny niche market. Money started to flow in and our circumstances began to change. Severn House was growing, we needed people to help us, and I had become pregnant with my first child, which Brian and I were very excited about. I was so busy commuting from our home in Wanstead, working in the office during the day and reading the books we were offered to publish in my evenings and at weekends, that I had no time to wonder whether I would enjoy being a working wife and mother. By then, it was time to move the company out of our respective homes. We were doing sufficiently well to take on office premises and Edwin found a suitable space at the top of a building in Bond Street. Before too long, there were eight of us working there together.

A year later, from the outside, my life looked brilliant. I owned half of a fast-growing, profitable publishing company with an office in Bond Street and a young, enthusiastic staff. I was capably managing the work–life balance of marriage, motherhood and career – although my husband and I were still adjusting to problems that had arisen at our daughter Sonia's birth, but we felt we would overcome them. I was earning good money and both Edwin and I were gradually becoming known and respected for our achievements. The fact that I had not gone to university might even have contributed to my life in a positive way, as I had used the years after school to gain valuable experience in the workplace. I was even able to offer to repay the £500 my father had loaned me to start the company. Graciously, he refused to accept it, telling me I might need to put it towards a deposit for the larger home that Brian and I hoped to buy in the not-too-distant future.

But underneath the surface things were not at all rosy. Edwin and I were both still in our twenties and now that we had a few years behind us as a start-up business, we were into the second phase of our growth. Building a company – hiring and managing staff and developing new systems – was uncharted territory for us, requiring a whole range of new skills. Neither of us had any management training and we both had different ideas about how the company should be run. There were a lot of long discussions, arguments and many differences of opinion, which we were unable to resolve. As both of us owned equal shares in the company, when we disagreed it was hard for us to reach a decision that we both felt was right.

The months went by and the company continued to do well, but the relationship between the two of us deteriorated sharply as we became financially more successful. I grew more and more depressed and was feeling like an imposter, questioning whether I was any good at what I was doing. I naively thought that if we were doing so well, we should be able to resolve our differences for the good of the company. I hated all the arguments we were having and how difficult it was to find solutions that we could agree on. It took many months of this unhappiness before the realization gradually dawned on me that I was no longer enjoying working in my own company. For a short time my life had shone with the brilliance of a diamond; now it felt murky and dark. My usual positive zest for life had completely disappeared. Everything had started out so well, but now I couldn't see how Edwin and I would ever fix our differences.

One morning, I woke up and, hating the idea of going to work that day, thought, "I can't do this anymore." I got dressed, went into the office and said to Edwin, "We can't carry on like this any longer. You will have to buy me out."

There was a great sigh of relief all round, from our families at home and from the office staff. A solution had been found to a very difficult situation and a decision was quickly made. With the help of our accountant, we agreed a valuation of the company and worked out a payment plan. Edwin would borrow more money from his family and would buy out my share of the company over a period of twenty-four months. I would be free to start another company if I wanted, but I could not publish any of the authors we had published at Severn House or those in our forthcoming programme.

In our last two years of working together, Edwin and I had not been able to get on, but now, with a clear resolution agreed upon, we were able to finalize my departure amicably – on good terms, though I felt bruised and battered by the experience.

And so, in the summer of 1978, after nine years in the workplace – four of them at Severn House – I found myself having earned the handsome sum of £50,000, which was my half-share of what we'd agreed the company was worth. In those days, the tax an entrepreneur had to pay when they sold their business was a much higher percentage of the sale than it is now. Nevertheless, there was enough money to live on for a while, which was very good news as, by then, my daughter Sonia was two years old and I had just become pregnant with my second child.

I was twenty-eight and felt completely washed up. I had worked tremendously hard for nearly decade and had experienced great highs and lows. I had loved growing the company, finding all the books to publish, reading them and persuading other people to buy them. I had enjoyed working as part of a team when times were good, and I had felt comfortable in the role of joint managing director. Edwin and I had enjoyed each other's company on a personal level but, ultimately, we hadn't been able to agree about the internal workings of the company nor what our future strategy should be.

My husband and I now had a sizeable mortgage. Another baby was on the way and Sonia, our first child, was growing up and her future was uncertain. There was every need to keep working.

What would I do next?

THREE
SONIA

During our life's journey, every one of us is likely to have one or two – sometimes more – catalytic events that will challenge us and perhaps even change the course of our lives and how we view the world around us. For me, the birth of my first daughter, Sonia, was to be one of those moments. Until then, my conventional life had not really had any unexpected twists or turns. I had grown up in what I thought was a regular suburban family with two parents and a younger sister. I had begun to build a career and had got married. Everything had followed an expected path. But now all that was to change.

I was twenty-six when Sonia was born. It is she who has been my greatest teacher in this lifetime. Everyone who becomes a parent embarks on a journey of great learning with their child. In my case, it was a journey for which both my husband and I were completely unprepared.

Sonia was a much wanted baby. At that time, I had been married for four years and was living in Wanstead, a pleasant suburb in East London. I had met Brian in my late teens and, after an on-off relationship lasting a couple of years, we had decided we were right for one another. We both wanted children and I had told him before we married that I did not want to be a stay-at-home mum.

Brian was, by then, working full-time as a chemist in the pathology department of the local hospital, which had the largest maternity unit for miles around. It had never occurred to either of us that we might go elsewhere for the birth. In those days there was much less knowledge about birth options and much less focus on the best possible experience for mothers.

When Sonia hadn't arrived a few days after her due date, I was advised to come into the hospital for an induced birth. It wasn't a great experience as I was left on my own for long periods of time during labour. Eventually, at around seven o'clock in the evening of 20 September 1976, Sonia arrived. She was so beautiful, with lots of lovely dark hair. We were both thrilled to meet her and to hold her in our arms. She was our very much longed for first child and we wanted for her the best life experience that we knew how to give.

The next morning, I woke up and she was lying peacefully in a little cot beside my bed. When a midwife came in and saw her and said she would take her away for a test, I didn't know how unusual that was. But then, a few hours later, we were told that Sonia was very ill. She had had a brain haemorrhage and was in intensive care.

It was such a shock. From great joy and happiness, we were plunged into immediate fear and despair. It was particularly tough on my husband, who had been working in the hospital's lab that morning. Suddenly it was all systems go, because there was a very ill baby in the intensive care ward. It was a terrible experience for him to discover that the baby was his own newborn daughter.

I was discharged from the hospital and sent home to try to express milk with a pump. I was advised to drink Guinness to help bring the milk in. The gorgeous little crib that my parents had bought for us lay empty in the newly decorated nursery. I didn't feel like talking to anyone and, in any event, my friends were all working. I didn't know what to do with myself. I couldn't even go to the hospital and sit by Sonia's bed for very long, as that wasn't allowed. My husband stayed at the hospital as he felt he was doing something useful there. It was such an unreal time.

We endured a fortnight of agony, and for the first few days we did not know whether Sonia would make it or not. It was a blur of visits to the hospital where Sonia had had her lovely hair shaved and was wired up to all kinds of beeping machines. I made endless, hopeless attempts at expressing milk. By now, the phone was ringing, as it was long past my due date; I had to go through the whole story over and over again, sharing it with friends and family who did not know what to say. Then, at last, the hoped-for good news. Sonia was doing better. She had turned the corner. She would be able to come home and our life with her could begin.

She had suffered a brain haemorrhage because, during labour, she had nearly strangled herself on the umbilical cord. I had known that something didn't feel right and had told the nurses that my pains were different from what I had been led to expect by the teacher at the NCT classes I had attended. It was only towards the end of the birth that they realized what was happening. Shortly after Sonia was born she had seemed to be in good health; it was only several hours later, when she was awake instead of sleeping, that the midwife had taken her away and raised the alarm.

We were told that, with any luck, Sonia would make a complete recovery. But there was a 25 percent chance she might not. All of us would just have to hope for the best.

I have always considered myself a fortunate woman, because for most of the time I have a fairly relaxed temperament and don't tend to worry overmuch. I figured that I would carry on as we had planned and I would go back to work at Severn House, leaving my daughter in the care of a nanny for three days a week at first, then increasing this to four. I had found a pleasant and experienced woman in her mid-fifties who lived nearby to look after Sonia. She was ready to wait a while to start work because she liked the idea of caring for a young baby. All the arrangements were in place.

Sonia came home and we did our best to smother her with love and affection to make up for her cruel start in life. We both loved her from the start, but of course we had not been able to bond with her straightaway. It took us all a while to get used to each other. Sonia was fairly placid but she could also quickly become upset and frustrated, and it was hard to know how to soothe her. She also seemed to be developing a little slowly, but when we took her at four months old to see the specialist, we were told to expect that. We were among the first of our family and our friends to become parents; we weren't meeting other babies and young children because we were both at work during the week, so it took us a while to realize that our experience was not typical.

It was only one day when Sonia was eight months old, when we had invited some friends to visit who had a child born two days before Sonia, that the difference in Sonia's development made itself clear. When our friends' sweet daughter picked up her bottle with both hands and drank her milk herself, Brian and I were shocked into silence. Sonia was not able to pick up her cup properly, let alone drink her milk from it, without support from us. Brian spoke to the specialist at the hospital, who said he would pop round to our home and see Sonia there. He was a very kind man, and it was good to be sitting in our own home and not in a bleak hospital consulting room when he gently broke the news to us that Sonia had cerebral palsy. He told us that she would not develop like other children and that we would not know how much she might develop – if at all – until many months had passed.

It took a while for the news to sink in. How could we have missed the signs that Sonia was not developing in the way that other children did? Had we had been in denial about her slow progress – or simply living in hope that she would in time catch up with the usual childhood milestones? Now we had to come to terms with a very different future for her from the one we had been hoping for and dreaming of.

My husband had a much more pessimistic nature than mine and I think he saw Sonia's disability as yet another challenging experience in his life that he would have to cope with. I, on the other hand, had always felt that things had gone right for me. I had always felt lucky: I knew that I was fortunate to have been born into a family with parents who were happy together, even though I didn't always get along with them. I had gone to a good school, had many friends, and had never lacked for anything. At the time, I was still enjoying my work at Severn House and felt lucky and privileged to be doing something so exciting. I therefore thought, "Why shouldn't something bad happen to me? I can't always expect to go through life without something happening that isn't what I want."

This balance of ideas and temperaments helped both of us to get up each morning and get on with the day. As the months passed and Sonia didn't really develop, we would be visited regularly by the friendly district midwife, who told us it was always a pleasure to come to our home and have a cup of tea with us, and that we were coping very well. Maybe she said the same thing to every young couple, but her support cheered both of us, and she always left us feeling that we did have some control of events. In reality, of course, we were in control of none of it.

FOUR

MY NEW COMPANY

In 1978, when I decided to sell my shareholding in Severn House to Edwin, Sonia was eighteen months old and Brian and I were hoping for a second child. I had absolutely no idea what the future would have in store for me. I only knew that I didn't have a choice. There had to be a better way of living than waking up feeling so miserable about going to work in my own company. After the sale negotiations were concluded, I felt freer than I had felt for a long time; a burden had been lifted from my shoulders.

While the negotiations were going through for the sale, Brian and I had made a momentous decision. Sonia had made little developmental progress since babyhood; she couldn't crawl, sit up or walk. It was hard for her to hold anything, not even a plastic cup or spoon, so she couldn't feed herself or easily play with toys. She was getting bigger and bonnier, turning into a beautiful child. She laughed and cried and made all kinds of sounds that indicated how she was feeling. She clearly had a sense of humour, but none of the noises sounded like words. She could do almost nothing of her own volition.

We had researched how we could help Sonia develop. Cerebral palsy is a form of motor disability that results from damage to the brain around the time of birth. Some people are only mildly affected by it, but Sonia had it very severely. We came across an unorthodox method of treatment for children with the condition, developed by an American neurologist, Temple Fay. It was controversial because there wasn't a great deal of evidence that it worked. Nevertheless, it was a programme that we could do at home and we felt we had no choice but to try it. We were shown how to work with Sonia's head and limbs, moving them in a variety of patterns that would simulate the development of a normal baby into a toddler and then a growing child. It was believed that this might activate Sonia's live brain cells to take on the additional function of the brain cells that had died when she had her brain haemorrhage. In that way, she might learn to move more than she was able to do at present. Secretly, of course, we were hoping she might in due course be able to crawl and then to walk.

The programme required a lot of time. We had to follow it for three hours a day, six days a week. Three people were needed to do it and then, as Sonia grew bigger, a fourth person would be required. Doing the "patterning", as it became known, was a massive commitment. Brian arranged to go to his lab in the late morning two days in the week and to make up the time by staying on in the evening. I had taken two mornings off work at Severn House; there was no question of my not working. By now, we had begun to understand more about the challenge of living with a disabled child and, however much I loved Sonia and wanted to be with her, I knew that we would always need plenty of help if we were going to have any quality of life at all when she grew older. I wanted us to have a happy family life and, as a mother, I wanted a happy life too. If the programme didn't work, Sonia would need 24-hour care for the rest of her life. We would need money to pay for that; for this reason, as well as my avowed intention to be a working mother, I never felt guilty about leaving Sonia at home with a nanny. For the time being, though, Sonia was getting plenty of attention and she was loving it.

We asked friends and family to help with the patterning. Some people thought what we were doing was wrong; others were so helpful and supportive that they will always have a special place in my heart. A local women's organization was very loving towards us and committed to help us on certain days of the week, arranging a rota to make it easier for us to find the helpful people we needed. They were so kind and generous with their time. Some of them loved Sonia so much.

After a few months of starting the patterning, I became pregnant again, which was wonderful news – we wanted Sonia to have a brother or sister. And just about the same time, I was able to make an important decision about my own future. My confidence had taken a huge knock in the last year of my time at Severn House: had things not worked out for me because I wasn't competent enough? At work I had rarely spoken about my home life. Like many working mothers of young children, both then and now, I always felt I had something to prove. There were still so few senior women in the workplace that most of us who were there had to work extra hard to show we were as good as, if not better than, all our male colleagues.

When I was sixteen, my parents had thoughtfully sent me to a careers guidance organization. I had filled in answers to reams of questions about what kind of person I thought I was and what I liked doing – making things, designing things, growing things, selling things. The information had been fed into a huge computer, which came up with the conclusion that I should have a career selling books. Neither the career counsellors nor my family had realized that publishing is about selling books. Aspiring to have a career as a bookseller had seemed to my family to fall into the category of being a shop assistant, such was the level of our ignorance about the knowledge required, and it wasn't given much more thought. Now I decided to consult the organization again as they had got it right the first time. This time, they suggested I might be suited to a career as a lawyer, which surprised me as I have never enjoyed reading legal documents or engaging in protracted negotiations. Happily, too, they reassured me that I was suited to the job of publisher and selling books and that, given a different set of circumstances, I might do very well and be happy.

I took their advice and registered a new publishing company. In the 1970s there were several highly respected publishing companies named after the individuals who founded them – William Collins (which later became HarperCollins), Weidenfeld, Victor Gollancz, and André Deutsch. I didn't yet have a grand vision of the business I wanted to build, but I decided I didn't want to hide behind a name that wasn't my own. I registered the company name Judy Piatkus (Publishers) Limited. In later years we changed it to Piatkus Books. This time, I was the sole shareholder and, after my difficult experience at Severn House, I intended to keep it that way.

It was November 1979 and I was four months pregnant with my second child when I embarked on the next phase of my entrepreneurial journey. My motivation was straightforward. All I wanted was to get up in the morning and enjoy myself doing work I liked. I needed to earn enough money to pay for help looking after Sonia and the new baby, to contribute to the mortgage and to avoid doing too much housework and cleaning, which I have always loathed. Earlier that year we had moved into a new house in Brook Road, Loughton, Essex. We had fallen in love with the house the moment we saw it. It had beautiful wood panelling in the hall and dining room, which gave it a lot of character. The kitchen and lovely square lounge were light and bright and looked out over a south-facing garden. The location was great, a few minutes from the high street and the Central line tube into town, and with beautiful Epping Forest on our doorstep. It seemed to us the perfect place to bring up our growing family.

Nowadays there is so much help and support for entrepreneurs who want to launch their own business. There's even a new word for it: a "start-up". But in the 1970s, it was very different. There were plenty of businessmen to talk to, but few businesswomen. Some men – including bank managers – had hardly ever met any senior business women in their working day or their industries. There were no obvious introductory business books to read, no classes or lectures to attend, no networks for women. If you were a businessman you could join a men's club in town or play golf or go to the local Rotary or Freemason meetings. If you were a woman you were not welcome at or invited to any of those gatherings. This situation remained largely the same well into the 1980s.

My experience of the publishing industry was based on what I had learned from the few junior roles I had held and from the experience I had gained at Severn House. But I had never been responsible for the finances or book production, so I had a very steep learning curve ahead of me. At least this time I knew it. What was more difficult was not knowing what else I needed to know that I hadn't yet realized I didn't know!

As soon as I opened my first Piatkus company bank account, I invested as much money as I could in my new venture, keeping back the bare minimum we needed for living expenses. I didn't know how long it would take before I could start drawing a salary, so I had to be very careful with every penny. My most important initial purchase was the latest and best typewriter on the market, the IBM Selectric – known as the "golf ball" owing to the round metal ball that printed the individual letters on the page. What made it such a treat was that it had a built-in self-correcting tape. Until that time, if you made a typing error, you either had to correct it with white ink, which looked messy, or you had to place a strip of white Tippex paper over the incorrect letter and hit the key again to erase it. If you were a typist prone to errors, like myself, it was all very messy and time-consuming. However, I was a fast typist after all those months at secretarial college and because I loved my new machine and was so proud of owning it, the typing I had to do became much less of a chore.

As I hadn't read any business textbooks, I didn't know that writing a business plan would be a good idea. Perhaps people weren't so obsessed with writing them at that time, and, in any event, I had a clear idea of what I needed to do in order to earn money. I would find new authors and new books to publish, and I would follow the process that we had used at Severn House. Edwin and I had agreed that I would not continue to work with any of the Severn House authors and that seemed perfectly fair to me. I planned to publish four novels a month in hardback and sell them to libraries. I would launch my first programme in September 1979. By then my second child – I didn't know whether it would be a boy or a girl – would be five months old. But, for now, there was something very pure about the idea of such a clean break and a beautiful empty desk.

The first thing I did was to ring up the publishers I had been working with at Severn House, tell them I planned to start my own company and ask if they would send me suitable books. Everyone was happy to deal with me, having worked with me before, and no one seemed to mind that I was working from home. Severn House had a good reputation for the integrity of our publishing. Very soon, potential books began to arrive in the post and every day there were exciting parcels to open. I treated myself to a limited edition early print by the artist Patrick Hughes and hung it on the wall above my typewriter. It showed a square brown paper parcel, partly unwrapped, with a multitude of rainbows coming out of it. That was how I felt as the post arrived every day. Which one of those brown parcels might turn out to be the one with the rainbow in it, the one that would lead to the crock of gold?

In the early 1980s, there was a new publishing trend. Previously, all novels had been published in hardback before they were released as paperback editions. Now, some of the mass-market companies were flexing their muscles and publishing commercial fiction straight into original paperback formats. As I was specializing in selling hardbacks to the library market, the paperback houses were happy to offer me these books, because my edition would not conflict with theirs in any way. The contract with the paperback company that licensed me to reprint in hardback also allowed me to sell to the book clubs.

I was so lucky – in the right place at the right time. I cannot remember all the novels that formed my initial publishing programme, but gradually my first catalogue came together. One of the most popular commercial genres for women at that time was gothic fiction. My first list contained novels from Virginia Coffman and Daoma Winston, two prolific American gothic novelists who had a track record in the libraries. The covers were easy to commission. Picture libraries supplied images of women in hooded cloaks set against backgrounds of night-time forests, castles, towers and dark woodland. Because the genre was so popular, photographers were producing plenty of images and it was easy to find inexpensive ones to use on our book jackets.

I had also been given sage advice about my company logo from Tom Woolston, the owner of one of the largest of the library wholesalers, on whom I was dependent for sales. I had travelled to Nottingham to meet him when I had decided to start my own company and he had advised me that having a powerful logo was key to getting my brand – or, in publishing terms, my imprint – effectively established in the library market. I needed to make sure my books stood out on the shelves.

I took his advice and went to Foyle's Bookshop in Charing Cross Road, at that time the largest bookshop in London. I studied all the books in the fiction department, observing the logos on the spines and how they stood out on the shelves. The imprint that attracted me the most was that of Four Square Books. Not surprisingly, the design was simply four small squares. I went ahead and commissioned a design with circles. When my own beautiful logo arrived, the design reminded me of a clover leaf without the stem. I am not a visual person and had not been able to imagine it myself when I'd briefed it, but I knew it was just right. I have to confess that it was not until very many years later that it was pointed out to me that the circles were shaped like the letter P with a short stem.

Over the years, many people would tell me what a strong logo I had. It had been commissioned well before the concept of branding was appreciated or understood in smaller companies, but it was tightly designed and easy to use and worked well on a book spine of any width. Before the internet, every publisher produced an attractively designed and printed catalogue, showcasing all their books, and a massive amount of printed material – brochures, showcards, display boxes, spinners. The logo worked well wherever it was used and it could be quickly identified when scanning the shelves in a bookshop. Later, we added the name Piatkus under the logo. Some of the larger publishing companies might have as many as thirty or forty imprints, especially if they have acquired smaller companies over the years, each of which becomes known for publishing a certain type of book. In the first few years of the company's existence, Piatkus became known for publishing good commercial fiction.

In the initial months of my new publishing venture, I was offered three brilliant authors who very quickly helped the imprint to become known. The first of these was a bestselling American novelist, Cynthia Freeman, who wrote cosmopolitan family sagas. The action in her books would move from New York to Rome, Paris and London. Stories about rich, sophisticated families were very popular in the 1980s. Everyone was watching *Dynasty* on television. Cynthia Freeman's books brought me a few rainbows, but the second author that I acquired brought a whole lot more.

I was sent the opening three chapters of a first novel, which was to be published as an original paperback. I rarely bought first novels by unknown authors for the libraries, but I knew immediately that this one was very special. The author had a powerfully mesmerizing voice and the plot was weird and original. I took a chance. The book sold and sold and was followed by three more in the series, all of them featuring the same characters and each becoming very successful.

My younger daughter was not born when I published the first of those novels. One day, many years later, when she was fourteen, she came home from school and said, "Mum, there's a novel I really want you to buy for me. All the girls in my class are talking about it."

"What's it called?" I asked.

"It's *Flowers in the Attic* by V. C. Andrews," said my daughter.

"Darling, I published it before you were even born!" I replied. It was such a thrilling moment for both of us.

Maybe you have never heard of *Flowers in the Attic*? But ask around your friends and it won't be hard to find a woman who read and loved the series as a teenager at school. (Although it was not originally marketed as a young adult novel, somehow over the years teenagers have adopted it for themselves.) V. C. Andrews was one of the top-selling novelists of the twentieth century and I was so lucky that I was able to publish her hardbacks on the Piatkus list so soon after the company's launch and before she became so famous. They sold very well in the libraries, and the book clubs absolutely loved them and kept reordering.

The book clubs were an important part of the growing business. They were a great way to reach customers who liked to own their own books and might not have had time to go to the local library. They also played an important role for those who liked to be guided in their selection, who wanted the book that everybody should be reading. Book clubs curated the best of all the new books and, because they could sell huge quantities of a single title, they were able to negotiate a high discount with publishers, which, in turn, meant that they could sell at a discount to their customers.

In spite of the high discount, we always loved selling to the clubs because it increased our print run (the number of copies we were able to print at one time) and brought down the cost of each volume. Very often, their reorders enabled Piatkus to keep a book in print for longer: we could reprint for the clubs and add on a small quantity for ourselves. They paid promptly, too – within sixty days – which helped our cash flow. The book clubs loved V. C. Andrews and we later produced attractive volumes especially for them, which contained all the books in the series.

The third American author who was offered to me at that time was Danielle Steel, a bestselling novelist then as she is now. She was offered to us by a publishing company called Sphere Books, who had published her first book in hardback but had decided to publish her in "original paperback" after that. Over the next decade, we were to publish more than ten of her new novels in simultaneous hardback, which would reprint regularly both for the libraries and the clubs. Another favourite rainbow author.

In the 1980s, public libraries were still a very important part of the community. WHSmith sold books, as did Boots and the popular downmarket high-street chain Woolworths, and the larger towns and cities had their own independent bookshops. But in those days, as mentioned earlier, the generous funding from local councils to libraries ensured they could acquire a wide range of new fiction, as well as lots of new non-fiction – a true delight for all prolific readers. We could sell several thousand copies of some of our authors to libraries, both in the UK and abroad. The work of promoting each of our three bestselling authors' novels was helpfully done by their paperback publishers, thereby driving many potential readers into libraries to borrow them. This helped put Piatkus on the map with our customers very quickly, even though we were new and small, and when we experimented with new authors, their sales would receive a lift from being on the same list as Cynthia Freeman, Virginia Andrews and Danielle Steel.

This success set the tone for our fiction for the next twenty-five years. We became known for what is described in the publishing trade as "downmarket" commercial fiction. These were books that were very much to my personal taste; I had always been an avid reader of popular women's fiction and now delighted in selling it with passion and enthusiasm. It was helpful that most senior fiction editors in many of our rival publishing houses preferred to publish upmarket literary fiction, keen to make their mark and build their careers through finding serious authors. In addition, the editors of the popular downmarket authors were often young women whose business acumen wasn't always taken as seriously by the male bosses and salespeople in their organizations as they should. At Piatkus, we were not aiming for reviews in the quality Sunday newspapers. We were simply happy to sell as many copies as we possibly could to as many readers as we could find who would enjoy these authors' books.

FIVE

LEARNING ABOUT NON-FICTION

For a whole year, I got up every morning and, after breakfast with Sonia, I would sit down at my typewriter and focus on creating the first publishing programme for my new company. By now, we had a live-in nanny who was looking after Sonia, and as I was never that interested in the running of the home, it was easy for me to be self-disciplined. In any event, now that we knew more about Sonia's condition, I was strongly motivated to make my company a good money-making venture.

Once or twice a week, I travelled into town to visit publishers and literary agents to comb their backlists for authors past their first flush of popularity, whose work I might be able to bring back into print. I would also find out which new authors the paperback publishers were bringing out. I had long been buying American fiction for Severn House and I decided I needed to make my first solo trip to America.

I loved reading American fiction, which seemed to me to be on a much wider, more imposing scale of writing than that of English writers, who would often set their novels against a backdrop of a small village or a few streets in the suburbs of a small town. Characters in American novels, I felt, were full of dramatic contrasts – often very rich or dirt poor, gangsters or sheltered young women from Waspy backgrounds. Descriptions of scenery ranged from vast forests of firs in the north to the palm-lined streets of Florida, or from the temperate coastal areas of California to the urban enclaves of New York and Boston. Even the novels set in small-town America seemed to me to be grander in scope than those set in our small English towns. It was good news for me that American fiction was not as beloved by many English publishers. British editors tended to want to find and develop their own home-grown talent. As I didn't have the skills of a hands-on editor, I loved to buy books on which someone else had already worked. They were much cheaper to produce as well.

I was pregnant with my second child in December 1978 when I flew to New York for the first time. I had never visited America before; the expense of travelling abroad was still a luxury for me and for many other people in the early 1980s. It was just before Christmas and I had been warned how cold it would be, so I had bought a voluminous white coat, which covered my bump. My mother had insisted I take a hat with me and I found a large furry one to match the coat. I felt like the Abominable Snowman but also virtuous, wrapped up against the cold. My mother was very worried about my trip. "It's such a dangerous place, New York. Must you go?" Of course, I paid no attention to her anxieties. A helpful London literary agent had recommended a women's hotel near Central Park. All the same, I had never travelled so far on my own, let alone gone abroad on a business trip for my new company. I was twenty-eight, excited and more than a little bit nervous.

New York is magical in December. Fairy lights everywhere, shop windows shining with light, and decorated Christmas trees glimpsed through doorways. It was all so beautiful. I had read so many novels set in the city. Arriving at night, it appeared everything a publisher of fiction could possibly have dreamed of. The hotel was situated on Sixth Avenue. I woke in the middle of the night, having no understanding of jet lag, and when I couldn't get back to sleep I sat up in bed and painted my nails. It was such a treat not to have to think about husband, children or anyone else but myself for a few days. I was already loving it.

That New York trip was to be the first of many. I always visited at least once a year and sometimes twice. Over the years, I built many wonderful relationships and discovered fantastic international bestselling books, some of which you may still have on your shelf to this day.

It was always easy to motivate myself to get out of bed and start work. I loved reading the books people were sending me and making offers to publish. However, there were certain areas of the business that Edwin had handled at Severn House and at which I was still a novice. We had regularly discussed the work that each of us was doing but we had established very clear boundaries for each of our roles. Now I had to find a printing company and negotiate terms. That wasn't so difficult because I had some guidelines from Severn House about what I ought to be paying. I also had to find a warehouse to look after the books and ship the orders – and that was much more of a challenge. The warehouse Edwin and I had used before was still being used by Severn House. It seemed best to try to find a completely different new home for my burgeoning range of books.

I knew that the publishing company Victor Gollancz had a warehouse and that it might be suitable for my new list. All I had to do was ring the owner of the firm, Livia Gollancz, and ask her if she might be interested in taking on my books as well. It was surely just a small thing, but I was petrified. Who was I to think I could call such a famous and eminent woman? I had never met her, she would not know who I was – she might not even speak with me. But time was getting short; I wanted to print my first catalogue and we needed an address to which library suppliers and customers would send their orders. Finally, I plucked up courage and made the call, and Livia was charming and very helpful. Her warehouse facility could not help me but she recommended a company in Littlehampton. Because of my previous experience, the managing director was happy to take the new list on. Suddenly people were wanting to help me, to smooth the road.

Having a good warehouse operation was very important, because not only would they store our books and despatch the orders – which would be sent to them direct by customers – but they also offered the facility to invoice our customers, collect the money for us and pay us within an agreed time. This meant that I would know several weeks in advance what income I could expect. All this was going to make my work so much easier; I would still have to pay close attention to the numbers, but I would have more control over the cash because I would know what was coming in and when. I would also be spared the very onerous task of organizing invoices and chasing the money owed to us. I knew nothing about accounting and although I'd had some basic lessons in book-keeping at secretarial college, I soon realized how much I didn't know. The first time I had promptly paid an invoice sent by my accountant, posting it back to him with a cheque attached, he had asked, "Why did you do that?" I hadn't realized I needed to keep a copy of each invoice for my own files. I was shocked at my level of ignorance.

Working from home enabled me to keep an eye on everything that was going on. I was able to continue with the "patterning" for Sonia, be very productive with my time and keep my overheads as low as possible. In my first year of trading, working by myself, the company turned over £180,000 and made a profit. I was very proud. It meant that I could stop putting all my savings into the company and could take some out in salary. I didn't discuss my finances with anyone except my accountant. The financial achievement seemed rather good, but I was of course wanting to do as well as we were doing at Severn House so I simply felt that I was on my way. I was more focused on what our publishing programme would be for the next year.

I have always believed that it is very important to start taking a salary from your business as soon as possible. You have to pay yourself first, factoring in all the time that you are working. If you don't allow a salary for yourself when you review your figures, then you are deluding yourself in thinking your business is a viable concern. You don't have to spend it; indeed, it's important to be very careful with your money when you are starting out. If you haven't spent all your salary and you run a bit short of cash in the business, you can always lend some of the money back to your company, as long as you can see that you will be able to return it to yourself within a short time-frame. I sometimes had to lend money back to the company as we grew, but by then I had paid tax on it, so I always made sure that the company returned all my short-term loans as quickly as possible.

Piatkus Books was growing and it was becoming clear that I would need to start hiring people to help me. June Laderman, a lovely lady in Loughton with whom I was friendly, offered to come and work as my assistant for two days a week. She was twenty years older than me and would be a steadying hand. She also put me in touch with Phyllis, a bookkeeper in her sixties, whom she knew from the local golf club.

My son, Matthew, had arrived in April 1979 a few months before our first books were published and two years later I was pregnant again. I loved working at home and didn't want to rent an office in the high street, so we had had to extend our house. At first, June worked in the spare bedroom and when Phyllis came to do the books she took over the dining-room table. But it had become clear that this arrangement could not last for long. With a third child on the way and a live-in nanny, the house would soon be overflowing, so we had embarked on the chaos of building first a loft and then a kitchen extension. As our overheads were low, the company was now generating a profit and I had been able to take a salary, which had contributed to paying for the building costs along with an extended mortgage.

The office in the loft was a beautiful, airy space with a solid staircase leading up to it. I visualized expanding the staff as the business grew. We would be able to fit six desks in there, along with bookshelves and filing cabinets. My third child, Leah, arrived in the middle of the kitchen extension being built. Luckily, it was July and warm weather, and she was a most obliging baby. I sat upstairs in the bedroom breastfeeding her while the builders continued their work downstairs. Somehow we all muddled through until it was finished.

As the fiction list developed and I got to know more and more people in the publishing industry, it was becoming clear to me that I would never be able to think of myself as a serious publisher unless I added some non-fiction to our publishing programme. I didn't read much non-fiction and I didn't know anything about publishing it, but as a fledgling entrepreneur I was realizing that I needed to keep challenging myself. I loved publishing novels but all the famous publishing houses whom I admired published both fiction and non-fiction.

We had produced a few non-fiction books at Severn House: television tie-ins in hardback and a few reprints of classic titles about aircraft and military matters, which Edwin had tracked down. It had never seemed like an area in which I would be able to get involved. Now, though, I began to discuss the idea with a few literary agents and think about the areas in which I might be interested. I liked books about cooking and the home and when I had been invited to review some general books of Jewish interest for a specialist magazine some years previously, I had enjoyed reading them. I wasn't sure if I knew very much about anything else. I didn't have huge life experience or much of a cultural education, aside from my Jewish heritage. I was running a business that involved reading novels and I had three small children. There wasn't a lot of time for anything else.

A literary agent offered me two cookbooks by a French master chef, Jean Conil: *Variations on a Recipe* and *Variations on a Starter*. The idea behind the series of books was that each spread would contain a page with one basic recipe while the one opposite would offer a range of variations to it. Julian Friedmann, the agent, recommended a designer, Paul Saunders, to help us create the pages and cover, and offered to share a stand with me at the next Frankfurt Book Fair so I would have a chance of selling foreign licences, which are also known as "rights" in the publishing trade.

I also found an intriguing American book called *Japanese Garnishes*, which contained four pages of colour photographs, several to a page, showing a number of intricate garnishes that could be created from vegetables such a cucumbers, radishes or carrots. The black-and-white diagrams and instructions filling the rest of the pages showed you how to recreate them in fine detail. The book would be easy to produce as I could buy the material I needed direct from the States and I would not have to do any work on the content myself. It would be like buying a reprint.

All I needed was an editor to help me with my fragile new list of books. I asked around; another literary agent mentioned a friend of hers who was looking for a job, and an interview was arranged at my home. I remember the first time Gill Bailey and I met. Tall and graceful, she arrived carrying a wicker basket that contained attractive books she had worked on for other companies. Always keen to look professional, I was used to carrying a briefcase everywhere and, being a complete townie, I was bemused by the contrast between us. We hit it off immediately, however, and it was agreed that she would come to the office two or three days a week to work in the loft and that she would work at home the rest of the time. Together we would find books and build a non-fiction list.

Gill had art school training and a background in producing illustrated books, although she hadn't edited whole texts before, so this would be a learning opportunity for her as well. We agreed she would also be responsible for briefing and commissioning the designers for the covers and insides of any books we published, although we would discuss them together beforehand.

This is how it was done in small companies in the 1980s. There were no psychometric tests, probably not even a second interview. Gill must have liked what she saw. Certainly I liked her and had confidence that she knew what she was doing.

Although we hadn't discussed it at our original meeting, it soon became obvious to Gill that she would be much more productive if she didn't commute to Loughton and could work from her home in North London. Already we were beginning to create the office of the future. Gill and I would meet up occasionally, but mostly we spoke on the phone two or three times a day. It was to be a long time before we worked together under the same roof. When the company was eventually sold, many years later, we were still working together. We had discussed every non-fiction book that Piatkus had ever published in fine detail. Gill was responsible for editing the British books we bought and I mainly acquired the American buy-ins, though I did read just about everything we published at some point. In the twenty-five years we worked together, there was rarely a cross word between us. We were always on the same page.

Authors loved working with Gill for her brilliance at editing, her generous guidance and encouragement, and her ability to bring out the best in them. She had an endless supply of patience. Many of our authors were experts in their subjects but not all were natural writers. Gill was unstinting in her devotion to the books Piatkus published – nothing was ever too much trouble.

SIX

BUILDING A COMPANY CULTURE

We were building a company and no one had told us how to do it. All I knew was that I wanted to publish good books and sell as many of them as possible for as long as we could. Growth was happening more by luck than by judgement or planning. My lovely first employee, June, continued to work for me. However, as we began to be offered more fiction and as the non-fiction list started to take shape in my head, I needed more help than a part-time assistant could offer and had gradually increased the number of people who were working for the company.

My very first employee was actually my live-in nanny. With full-time support from her, I knew I would be able to offer my children and husband the best of myself in the hours I had with them each day. Because I worked at home when the children were young, I was around in the mornings and frequently at other times of day if I was needed. There was little faraway travel for work – only my occasional visits to key customers, and my annual trips to America and the Frankfurt Book Fair. In the 1980s, households were not organized so much around children's lives and their needs in the way they often are now, and I never felt guilty about time spent away from them. When I was away, Brian and the children's nanny always looked after them well, and they saw a great deal of both sets of grandparents. We also did a lot of home entertaining on the weekends, making lunches and teas for friends who would visit us with their children.

Now that I had my own company, I had the freedom to manage my own hours. With mobile phones and computers still a very distant dream, it was easy to have a clear boundary between home and work. I would finish work at about five o'clock and spend time with the children. Their nanny would give them supper and after they were in bed and Brian and I had eaten dinner together, my working hours continued while I sat in an armchair, next to which a pile of typescripts submitted to the company would always be waiting for my attention.

Aside from spending time with people you love, most of us want to use our lives to do meaningful work, to use those talents with which we have been born. If, as a parent, you can manage your own time as well as possible, you will then be able to lead a more stress-free existence. I believe that being able to organize your own time is the most important key to freedom in the workplace.

In the 1980s, it was legal for a family nanny to be an employee of a company and it was possible to buy your car through your company without it being taxed as a benefit in kind. My first year of running Piatkus was very profitable because the only employees were myself, June and the nanny. There were two breadwinners in the house – still not the norm for many families with young children in the early 1980s. After the mortgage and living expenses had been paid, we had a little left over and, in addition to our family saloon, we were able to treat ourselves to a little Triumph TR7 sports car. We didn't know how long we would have it, but we thought we would enjoy it while we could.

Prior to Gill joining the company, my first full-time employee was a friendly and easy-going young woman called Dorothy, later Mrs Hounam, who lived in nearby Buckhurst Hill and joined us just after the company celebrated publication of its first list in the autumn of 1979. I was still working from my bedroom when she accepted the job of my assistant and we assembled a desk for her in my baby son's bedroom, which, luckily, was fairly large. Dorothy loved children and didn't mind the noise and commotion that were part of the experience of working in our house. She soon mastered the job and I felt confident about promoting her to be in charge of sales.

We hadn't needed sales representatives for the library fiction market, but when we launched our new non-fiction list we appointed a team of freelance reps, who began to sell our books into the major accounts, including WHSmith, and to the wholesalers who supplied many of the independent bookshops.

In those days, most bookshops were independents, and much of a bookseller's day was spent seeing salespeople. Dorothy began to visit accounts in London and our handpicked team sold our books in other parts of the country and in Ireland. With Dorothy on the road, I realized I would need another assistant to deal with the growing mountain of administrative tasks. We were buying more books, so there were more contracts to negotiate, more letters to answer and general paperwork to deal with. Every communication had to be typed by hand and the phone rang constantly.

In the 1980s, ideas about company culture were unknown to most people. A managing director's traditional way of managing was still hierarchical. But I had my own ideas too. Earlier in my career I had worked for one company that had been very political. People were always running in and out of each other's offices, closing doors and sharing secrets. As a young secretary, I had wanted to know more about what was going on and, owing to those closed doors and politicking, it had taken me a long time to learn how the company worked. At Severn House, the problems had been different but no less difficult; the escalating tensions between Edwin and myself had affected everyone. Now I had my own company and I was determined to be happy coming to work each day. I recognized that in order to achieve my goal, everyone else would need to be happy too. I had to learn to combine a natural tendency to give orders with my deeply-held desire to work in an office with no politics. Later, I realized that every office has politics and that it is only possible to minimize this when there is trust between all the stakeholders. Openness, transparency and honesty in everyone's dealings, both internally and externally, would be essential to achieve this.

Everyone wants to get up each day and feel that their work has a purpose, that who they are and what they do matters to everyone else they work with – in the case of publishing, with the shareholders, staff, authors, freelancers, suppliers and customers. Everyone involved with the company at every level needs to know that they count as individuals, that they are not just "bums on seats", only there to make money for the top management and shareholders. The actions and interactions of management – not what you say but what you actually do – are the ways in which you create trust. So many top corporate managers say one thing to their staff but behave in a completely different way themselves. You can't have trust within an organization when that happens; you can't state your values on your website and allow them to be at odds with what you yourself are actually doing. Your own behaviour must always be in alignment with the values of your enterprise. It is your actions that count. As a leader, you have to "walk your talk" and you have to do that every moment of every day.

This is not to say that in the twenty-eight years of Piatkus's history we always got it right. Of course we didn't. Managing people's expectations is always very hard, especially so in creative businesses. But we did come from a place of wanting to get it right and I believe that is why, over the years, we had such a low turnover of staff and were able to retain so many key people and create a lot of genuine goodwill. This is not to say that I understood all this then with such clarity, and especially not always in the early days when the quick temper of my youth and inexperience sometimes got the better of me. Nevertheless, I always did care about the people I worked with, and, at some level, most of them knew it and felt it; they were more inclined, as a result, to forgive my occasional temperamental outbursts, which did lessen as I became a more experienced manager.

In the 1980s, I don't think I ever considered going on a course to learn to manage people better; I am not sure many existed. But by the 1990s, we had begun to publish self-help books and a whole new world opened up for me. Nowadays, people go on management courses to learn how to get the best out of colleagues. But, in truth, if the culture of your company is not one of deep respect for other people, there is not a great deal that going on a course can help you with. You will know the right thing to do, but if you are not able to do it because the heads of your company do not encourage or allow it, you will not feel good as you look at yourself in the mirror every morning. You may struggle each day as you come face to face with the person you are at work, which may be so different from the person with integrity you want to be – and indeed may already be – in your heart.

Our small, very happy little team moved into the loft extension. I moved the Patrick Hughes print of the parcel with the rainbows from my bedroom and would continue to look at it every morning as I opened the post. What might I find that day in one of the varied assortment of parcels and jiffy bags that were now arriving in increasing quantities? Gill and I would send regular parcels between us by messenger and by now I had not only taken on June and Dorothy but also the local doctor's daughter, Jane Burton, who was to be with the company for more than twenty years. Eventually, Jane knew the answer to just about everything. "Ask Jane" became a familiar refrain over the years.

One day in 1981, after three years of building the company, I answered the phone to Philip Cotterell, who had joined Severn House about eighteen months before I'd left and had been responsible for sales. We had always got on well and I had rung him occasionally to ask his advice as I embarked on the challenge of visiting key customers myself. Philip had recognized the strong ambition within me to build my own successful company and, now that three years had passed, he could see we were beginning to create books that were sufficiently distinctive to stand out in a crowded marketplace. He was ready for a new challenge and wanted to meet up.

The conversation turned to the future of Piatkus Books. We were growing fast, and needed more sales expertise if we were ever to achieve the ambitions we had to become global. Suddenly he and I were discussing his joining the company, becoming responsible for all our sales, both home and export, with Dorothy, as sales manager, reporting directly to him. As I hadn't written a business plan, I hadn't envisioned what my future sales department might look like; I had only focused on the books we had just published and those in the pipeline, and the beautiful creation that was growing inside me because I was pregnant at the time.

At first I had misgivings. "Are you sure you will feel comfortable working in our loft with the children and their nanny in the house?" Philip wasn't concerned about that, but I couldn't help feeling a little apprehensive. I knew that my management skills still needed to develop. How would he fit in with this company of women? Up until then, all of us had been rubbing along very well and, even though June was part-time and Gill still worked from home, we were achieving a great deal as a team.

In the end, Philip joined Piatkus several months after my third child, Leah, was born in July 1981. At the time of our initial discussion, a new nanny had just started and I had been eight months pregnant. The kitchen extension was just being finished and there was dust and rubble and chaos everywhere. If he wasn't fazed by all of that, I decided he could cope with anything.

As it turned out, I need not have worried. Like Gill, Philip was very flexible in the way that he worked and he too had a publishing background, having worked for several different companies both in the UK and in Australia. He didn't have to come into the office very much. He needed to be out there meeting people, selling books and building our profile, and he turned out to be extremely good at it. He was an excellent and enthusiastic salesperson, very good at strategic thinking and negotiation. He also had a special talent for understanding the various export markets into which we wanted to expand.

While I enjoyed and was good at selling, I had realized by then that I was a natural-born entrepreneur, temperamentally suited to engaging with the different challenges that regularly arose. I was not afraid of risk. I took decisions and I liked solving problems. I wanted to build a sizeable company and I was comfortable in that role. Without realizing it at the time, in Gill and Philip I was already creating the dream team. We all had a clear understanding of the direction in which we were headed and each of us knew what our responsibilities were. I was only too delighted to have as my colleagues lovely people who were much better at their individual roles than I could ever be. I trusted both of them and, while we all discussed the progress of the work together, I left them to get on with their tasks while I got on with mine. We were, without realizing it, creating the forerunner of the office of the future, a hub where employees did not need to be present in the same physical place every day. We spoke often by landline telephone – the only method of communication then – and sometimes all came together for a meeting. It was working just fine.

SEVEN
PROGRAMME BUILDING

There's a saying that "fortune favours the brave". All entrepreneurs need vast amounts of courage to build a solid company, because constant uncertainty is your daily companion. You get used to living with it, knowing that it ebbs and flows, so that, over time, you start to feel a little safer as you come into work in the morning and sit at your desk surrounded by your creation. But you can never relax entirely. The moment you begin to rest on your laurels you are done for, because the market takes no prisoners.

Severn House had been a straightforward business because we were not creating new books. As long as our main customer – the libraries – continued to have a local government budget with which they could buy our titles, and as long as we continued to work closely together with our customers to ensure we were giving them the authors they wanted to buy, we could stay in business. The work of conception and editing and sales and marketing of the books we published had been done by others many years previously.

Successful book publishing – and indeed successful manufacturing of any kind – is all about creativity. You are either the creator of the object or you are working with the creator – in our case, the author – and you are bringing to life an object that did not exist before. You have a completely free hand in how you conceptualize, design and present this object to the world.

I always felt that creating a non-fiction book was a much more complex product than many of the items that our customers might choose to spend their money on. If you looked at a glass or a piece of china, it was two-dimensional. We not only had to get the size and shape of the book (known as the "format"), the cover and the pricing right, but the content inside had to be of the highest quality and fulfil expectations. I always felt we were working in three dimensions.

As we developed, expanded and built our range of books, I would think of our typical customer as a woman – most of our books were aimed at women – with a limited amount of disposable income in her purse. She may have had a £10 note in there (the use of credit cards only started to become commonplace during the 1980s) and she didn't really want to spend more than that on a book. Every bookshop was stocked with thousands of titles; an average independent bookshop might have had as many as 30,000 books in it. Our task as publishers was to persuade this female customer to open her purse and purchase one of our titles. It had to look sufficiently enticing, both inside and out, that she would be prepared to take it to the till, pay for it and walk out of the shop with it. I did not see our competition only in terms of other books. I viewed it as everything else that hypothetical woman could have spent her money on – food, shelter, clothing, entertainment, a cup of coffee with a friend. Of course this mythical customer was only going to purchase our books if they were in the shop in the first place. This was the 1980s, and online purchasing of books was not to begin to affect the trade seriously for almost another twenty years.

We therefore determined from the start that we needed a very clear reason for each non-fiction book to come into existence. We had to create something that did not already exist and we had to be able to give the bookseller a good reason to stock it. Every time we evaluated a book, we would ask ourselves who the likely customer for the book would be and why anyone would buy it. It is always harder to convince a large customer to stock your products when you are a smaller company. We needed the bookseller to immediately understand who the customer would be for that book. Unbeknownst to us, we were developing our own concept of USP – unique selling proposition – something that is now taught in the first lesson of every entrepreneurship course. A company's USP is the unique factor or characteristic that distinguishes it from other organizations of a similar nature. But we hadn't been on any such courses; I didn't have a mentor – there wasn't anyone to teach us. We learned by listening to people and by experience.

This lack of expert knowledge had its advantages in that we had to work everything out for ourselves. We were lucky we were able to do so before we got into deep trouble. The lessons were hard won but also very simple. If we got a book wrong, we – or rather I – would lose money; when we got it right, we would make money. We simply had to get more books right than wrong and we could stay in business. We didn't know until quite a long time later that it would be a good idea to analyse our figures in detail to see how much each book had earned for us or how much money it had lost. When we did that exercise, there were often lessons to be learned. What we did learn, though, and fairly quickly, was that when we didn't get it right we would be left with a pile of stock that we had paid for and which would sit in the warehouse. And no one – not even jobbing merchants – would ever want to buy any of it. In the days before charity shops sold books on the high street, when you had truly got the concept of a book wrong you couldn't even give it away.

I was courageous – though such a thought never occurred to me at the time – and I was also very lucky. Had I started my publishing company just a few years later, it would have been far harder to get it off the ground. For an entrepreneur, timing is everything and you rarely have any control over that. Piatkus Books was founded at the beginning of a decade of great change in the publishing industry. At the start of the 1980s, there had been publishing companies that published either hardbacks or paperbacks. When the hardback companies sold paperback companies a licence to publish a book, they kept half the income from the paperback companies and divided the other half with the author. But during the 1980s, most of the major English-speaking hardback and paperback houses on both sides of the Atlantic realigned themselves to form new, enlarged, global organizations that could publish a book in both hardback and in paperback editions. These vibrant new publishing houses were now making much greater profits. They didn't have to share so much income with authors, so the amounts they could pay upfront for the authors they wanted began to climb and then to soar. They were also able to spend much more money experimenting with new and exciting forms of marketing. By the end of the decade, smaller publishers such as ourselves had become priced out of the marketplace. We could no longer compete for the best authors or finance the substantial marketing budgets that came with them.

When I had had launched the company at the beginning of the 1980s, popular authors did not get paid so much. While we at Piatkus Books were not well enough known to be offered many authors' books directly, if we came up with a good idea, we felt sufficiently confident to approach any author whom we wanted to write it. If the author liked the idea, and as long as we could offer them an amount of money that everyone considered fair, they would be happy to work with us.

The subject of food and drink was an obvious area for a mother of three small children to explore. As I worked from home and there was no commute, I wasn't usually too tired to cook. I only prepared simple quick dishes for main weekday meals, but I did particularly like baking for family teas on the weekend. Baking was good active form of relaxation at the end of a day at the typewriter. I had several cookbooks with simple lunch and supper recipes in them. What I didn't have was a book of quick cake recipes and I thought how lovely it would be if such a book existed. I would be able to put all the ingredients in my new food processor, whizz them together and quickly pop the cake in the oven. I wanted a whole book of recipes like that. Who could create it for us?

There had always been cookery programmes on television. At the time of my cake hunger, the most popular baker on television featured in an afternoon programme. Her name was Mary Berry. I invited her literary agent out to lunch, putting the idea to her, and she said she would ask Mary if she was interested in writing the book. I named the highest advance we could afford – our payment to the author, which would be set against the royalties that she would continue to earn if the book sold well. Mary liked the concept and agreed to do it.

Cookbooks in the early 1980s did not need to be heavily illustrated and lavishly designed in order to sell well. Very often the books had several recipes on each page and some ran over the page, so you had to keep turning the pages backwards and forwards while you were cooking – which was annoying. We decided that each recipe would be on a separate page or on a double-page spread so that the book would be easy to use in the kitchen. To illustrate the book, we had to hire a cook and food stylist for three days and rent the use of a photographic studio. Some photographers specialized in food and drink and they owned a lot of china and glass, which we could borrow. Both Gill and I went to the shoot. I am not a visual person so it was more for the excitement of the experience that I went, rather than for any wisdom or culinary expertise that I would be able to contribute.

Fast Cakes was published in 1981 and quickly established itself as one of the most popular baking books ever. We made one small mistake in the first edition of the book. For some reason the words "3 large eggs" were left off the ingredients list for the cherry cake. Although we corrected it in the next edition, for quite some time afterwards our receptionist would receive anguished calls from women in the middle of making the recipe who couldn't work out why the mixture wasn't turning into a batter. We reprinted the book many times in the next few years.

We later sold the paperback rights and it stayed in print until just a few years ago, when it was amalgamated with its sequel, *More Fast Cakes*, into one volume. I have no idea how many copies we sold but all of us involved with the book were very happy, including Mary herself. She was the easiest and most professional of authors to work with. Together we made a good team and for the next decade Mary created more books for us in what was to become a "Fast" series. Later on, we created *Mary Berry's Cookery Course* and *Mary Berry's 250 Favourite Recipes*, which were also to sell extremely well for us.

Alongside Mary Berry, there were a couple of other well-known names who gave our company credibility in the first few years of our life. One of those was the BBC's correspondent in Jerusalem, Michael Elkins, whose distinctive American voice was frequently heard booming from the radio. On my second trip to the States, I was in a large bookshop scanning all the titles, looking for something interesting that I might be able to publish in England, when I came across a book by him called *Forged in Fury*. Surprised that I hadn't heard of it, I read it and was enthralled. It was a rather uneven, passionately written book containing stories of people who had died in concentration camps and a plot to poison the water supply of a German city. It was based on true experiences yet had all the storytelling narrative and drama of the darkest of thrillers. Without enquiring too closely as to why no one else in England had wanted to publish it – we later found out that publishers had been put off by its unconventional structure and had been concerned the stories might not be entirely true, undocumented as they were – I asked the American publisher if we could license it for our non-fiction list.

I was thrilled with my find. We published in hardback with a higher price point than was usual for us because this wasn't a book just for women. (When men want to buy a book, they don't care about the price. They just take it straight to the checkout.) We were very excited about the sales prospects as we knew there would be a sizeable Jewish market for it. Our first print run was an ambitious 5,000 copies in hardback. Some of the central London bookshops would not stock it, suspicious of a book by Michael Elkins coming from Piatkus. This was not a genre of book that we had published before and it was by a well-known broadcaster. If *Forged in Fury* was so good, why wasn't a larger company publishing it?

Review copies were sent out to all the major newspapers. One Sunday morning I got an unexpected call from my father: "Your book has got a huge review in the *Sunday Express* this morning!" My parents very rarely asked me about my work, but this time my father sounded rather impressed. I ran out to the newsagent in the high street to buy a copy of the paper. The literary reviewer, Graham Lord, had been gripped by the book and gave it a marvellous review. Our total print run sold out within a week. We even had the very famous and upmarket bookshop Hatchards of Piccadilly on the phone, begging us for copies.

Forged in Fury should have put us on the map as a publisher to take notice of, but there wasn't a national bestsellers list in the 1980s. Reporters would ring round a few bookshops and ask what was selling well, and if a publisher owned the bookshop – as a few did in those days – they would often suggest their company's titles. *Forged in Fury* didn't raise our profile in the book trade as much as we would have liked, but it did sell a lot of copies and we reprinted it several times. A few years later, we sold the paperback rights and continued to receive royalties from that edition, too, for a long time afterwards. Years later, on occasion, if I visited the home of a new friend, I would very often see the distinctive red, black and white colours of *Forged by Fury*'s spine on their bookshelf.

Another well-known personality with whom we worked in the first few years of the company was Melvyn Bragg, who was fronting *The South Bank Show*, the best culture programme on UK television at that time. We had come up with an idea for a series of books for beginners about different aspects of culture and approached him to be the series editor. Our first book turned out to be the one that had the longest life – *How to Enjoy Poetry* by Vernon Scannell.

After a couple of years, we were beginning to build a solid reputation for books of Jewish interest, in addition to our list of titles targeted at women. We were creating our own niche in the marketplace and began to be offered an increasing number of projects via literary agents and American publishers, as well as suggestions for new books from authors themselves who had read and heard about our books. We were also enjoying experimenting with different formats and textures for covers. We wanted our books to be displayed front of shop and to stand out.

The 1980s were a popular period for all kinds of gift books and there were far more gift shops on high streets than there are now. We launched a gift book line of small hardback books at low prices. The first was *The Little Green Avocado Book*. Avocados were fairly new on greengrocer and supermarket shelves at the time and people didn't know what to do with them. We were thrilled to get an initial order for a thousand copies from a company who wanted to use the books for a promotional deal.

This popular title was soon followed by "Little Books" on garlic, peppers, lemons, apples and strawberries, and we created a small display box to sit by the till which proved very popular with the bookshops. *The Little Strawberry Book* was written by Leah S. Matthews, my pseudonym that encapsulated the names of my three children. I enjoyed writing it – it felt like a school project – but it was a lesson to my ego when it sold many fewer than the other titles and became the only one in the series that didn't reprint. Every "Little Book" had a first printing of 20,000 copies – with *The Little Book of Tea* and *The Little Book of Coffee* selling particularly well – because by then we were also able to sell the series through specialist gift wholesalers in the UK, as well as to the export market. They were very touchy-feely, and people loved having a whole row of them on their shelves at home. It would be very hard to publish these small, inexpensive books nowadays; everything is sold online at discounted prices and it is impossible to translate their attractive touchy-feely appeal to the computer screen.

We also published *Sonia Allison's Biscuit Book* in a horizontal format, which had a cover designed as a shortbread biscuit, and *Sonia Allison's Sweets* book, which emulated a chocolate bar. During the next few years we experimented with gift books on pancakes, pizzas, sausages, cats, roses and several other titles. We even launched a separate imprint called Diamond, which was for illustrated gift books. They were fun to do and we didn't lose money on many of them but, in time, we realized that highly illustrated gift books weren't really our forte and, with regret, we decided to stick with the more conventional book formats for the time being.

EIGHT
LEARNING NEW THINGS

All the time during my working life as a publisher, I was learning. Books and typescripts piled up on my desk every day. There were sample chapters of non-fiction, each chapter stapled together, with carefully constructed cover letters and synopses telling us about their contents, and bound book proofs sent from publishers in America; and sometimes authors simply wrote in, asking if we wanted to see their work before going to the expense of posting it. All this material had to be dealt with and reviewed and responded to. At first there was just Gill and myself reading everything; during most of the years of my career as a publisher I read at least two or three books each week. The pressure to keep reading was always relentless, even as the company expanded and we were able to take on more staff.

I loved coming into my office every day and never knowing what magic might be in my in-tray. Every now and again, there was a novel by one of my favourite authors, whoever that might be at the time. I rarely knew what was coming when. An agent would say, "My author is hoping to finish it this autumn", or an author would say, "You will get it after Easter." If there wasn't a contractual deadline – or even if there was – I never knew from day to day what might arrive in the post. Some material was addressed to me personally by authors who didn't yet have or didn't want to use an agent. Sometimes I remembered their names because we had seen their work before and written them an encouraging note. Authors were requested to send in a stamped envelope or jiffy bag if they wanted us to return their material, and we always had a large number of parcels to pack and post.

I had realized by then how much pleasure it gave me to share the new novels and the new non-fiction we were publishing. Every time I met with a business colleague or visited a friend, I would think beforehand about what they might like to read and would take a copy of that book with me to give to them. While of course it was important that every new book we created sold as many copies as possible, it gave me huge pleasure to know we were often birthing new thinking into the world. I loved it when people sent me proposals for non-fiction. New ideas always intrigued me and even if I couldn't see how we could turn many of them into successful books, it was always interesting to think about a topic from a new perspective. Books have so much power to entertain and to transform all our lives.

Every author sent us their work in the hope we would want to publish it, and we always respected that and tried to respond as appropriately as we could. Many people knew very little about the process of publishing, but they had read other books that we had published or they had read about our company and they liked the sound of us. If we had been featured in the media that week, if I spoke at a writer's group or on the radio, or if one of us met someone somewhere who was writing a book, we would often receive an extra-large postbag shortly after the event. In the publishing industry, unagented books that are offered direct to publishers – unsolicited manuscripts – join what is traditionally called "the slush pile". Every day, when untended, it gets higher and it was usually the task of a junior editor to go through it after their other work was completed. It is rare to find a publishable book in the slush pile; it is like finding a diamond in a haystack. Many of the larger houses ask people not to send in unsolicited submissions as they don't have enough qualified staff to read them all.

I believe that everyone does have a story inside them, a story that they want to tell, a story that is bursting to come out. But, at the same time, that doesn't mean there is necessarily a large enough market out there, keen to read their work, to make publishing it a commercial prospect. What made me saddest of all about the slush pile was when we would receive a whole book written by someone who did not know how to write English properly. They may have been educated in this country but for whatever reason – poor teaching, poor learning capacity, dyslexia – they were unable to write in grammatical sentences, which made their work unreadable. I always found it heartbreaking to see the effort that had gone into the work and to know that this person might well have a wonderful story inside them, but they did not have the basic writing skills to be able to share it. Early on in the history of the company we had more time to look at the slush pile as we weren't getting offered so many books. We knew that many authors did not understand how publishing worked and that it would be helpful to them to try to find an agent.

We did occasionally discover authors whose work we liked so much that we went on to publish not just their first book but several books after that. What was difficult sometimes was if the author then found themselves a literary agent who didn't know our company well enough and wanted them to move publishers. If the agent decided that we were not the publisher they wanted for their client's future work, in spite of there always being an option to offer us their next book written into the publishing contract, there would often be little loyalty. It is an occupational hazard for all publishers, no matter their size, when authors change agents.

We were not just in the business of publishing authors, but we were also there to manage their expectations and to keep them happy. We were putting our own money on the line to publish their work. But some authors were never going to be satisfied, whatever we did. If their future ambition was to be published by one of the famous larger companies, there was nothing we could do about it. We would simply carry on building their sales and reputations, knowing that one of our competitors might end up reaping rewards from our endeavours. We did love it, though, when authors told us that being published by Piatkus had turned out to be far better than being with a larger house, as the experience was so much more personal at every stage of the process.

In 1983, a book was offered to us that was truly a veritable rainbow. My understanding was that it had landed on my desk because no other British publisher wanted it. The book was *Colour Me Beautiful* and it had been published by a small company in the States and had become a huge bestseller. It was to sell in huge quantities for us over the next few years and launch a whole new genre of books. Its author was Carole Jackson, who believed that each woman would look her best in the colours that suited her most. All that woman had to do was to make better choices about the colours she wore.

Carole categorized each woman according to the four seasons. To find out the season that was right for her, each woman would hold a colour palette made from one of four ranges of coloured materials in front of her face and see which suited her best. With my dark hair and olive complexion, I was clearly a Winter: I looked good in deep colours with a background shade of blue in them. Gill was a redhead, an Autumn, who looked her best in leafy russet reds, browns and autumnal greens. We instantly knew this book was ground-breaking, offering women a completely new approach to exploring how they looked. Not only that, but Colour Me Beautiful consultants were popping up everywhere in the States: women in search of a new career where they could choose their own hours and work from home. We had to hope and trust that the revolution would spread to the UK in the same way.

We were lucky to have found ourselves an extremely talented freelance publicist. Jana Sommerlad had come to the UK from Czechoslovakia as a young woman and had married an Englishman, who had a very senior position as a television news producer. Like me, she was a mother of small children; PR enabled her to fit her working life around them. Jana was and continues to be a real powerhouse. She worked so hard on all our books and was so diligent at following up leads. Her polite but firm persistence was legendary both inside the company and with all those whom she dealt with in the media. We were constantly challenging her commercial acumen by presenting her with books on subjects that were new to the marketplace and which were hard to promote, but she took everything in her stride and never failed us. I used to think of her as our company's "secret weapon", so precise was her targeting of the right media outlets for all our books.

It was decided that we would publish *Colour Me Beautiful* in September, always a good month for a launch, the beginning of the autumn shopping season for both clothes and books. We held a media press conference at which the UK's only colour consultant at the time demonstrated how the system worked. Four of us from the Piatkus office, each with different complexions, stood bravely onstage as the range of different coloured materials were draped in front of us. As a publishing house, we were offering something new – and that did attract the attention of the media. However, there was a mix of good and bad reviews. I remember opening the *Observer* newspaper magazine, where a popular columnist tore into the whole idea, describing me as wearing a dress in a "gasworks grey" colour, and saying the whole idea was ridiculous.

Nevertheless, in spite of the cynicism with which many people greeted the idea, the force of *Colour Me Beautiful* was unstoppable. Gradually the book and the organization took off. Colour, image and style consultations became very popular as birthday and Christmas gifts, and women went shopping in the high street with their little colour palettes clutched in their hands. *Colour Me Beautiful* influenced the fashion industry as well. Where once clothes had been displayed according to their size, now they were styled according to colour. It was possible to go into a shop and see immediately if there was something that might suit you.

NINE

WORKING MUM

The time flew past and suddenly Piatkus Books had been trading for nearly five years. The loft extension was a huge success and everyone enjoyed working there. Our cleaning lady, Doreen, began to work extra hours – not to clean, but to pack parcels; she would sit at the kitchen table packing up piles of typescripts and books. Even the children and their nanny did their bit, walking to the local high street every day and queueing in the post office to send the parcels off.

I often took the opportunity to go to the post office as well, to get out of the house for some fresh air. At first, I would push Sonia and then, as the family grew, Sonia and Matthew would be seated side by side in the double buggy; and then Sonia and baby Leah would sit there while Matthew walked alongside. There was something about the atmosphere in the post office that Sonia hated. We would go inside and stand in the queue and after a while she would get bored and start shouting. Perhaps she simply wanted to be on the move again. I would frequently hear the refrain "you've got your hands full" as we hurriedly exited to carry on with our shopping, trying to get the buggy into yet another shop with doors that were only just wide enough.

We had continued with the patterning until Sonia was offered a place at a lovely, nurturing nursery school for disabled children in Harlow. During the time that we worked with Sonia on the patterning, it had gradually become evident that although she moved her limbs more easily, she hadn't made the improvements in her being that we had hoped. She was still unable to speak or move very much of her own volition. She could grasp a toy for a short period, but then it would fall out of her hand and she would not be able to pick it up again. She could not feed herself or sit – unless propped up. We did not see any evidence that she would ever be able to walk. A school bus picked her up every morning and she was returned home in the afternoon. Sonia has always been able to express her feelings through a variety of different sounds and we knew she liked the school because she was always happy to be lifted onto the bus in the morning and she used to return to us in a good mood.

For now, we were happy she was settled and I chose not to think about her future. I didn't devote any time to worrying what our lives might be like in five, ten or fifteen years. Sonia grew bigger and taller and, gradually, heavier. We could carry her upstairs, hoisting her in a fireman's lift over our shoulders without too much difficulty, and we could move her around the home, lifting her in and out of her chair, the bath, or the car. She was unable to assist us by putting her arms around our necks, so she usually felt like a dead weight and we had to be careful she didn't slip and slide through our fingers. We looked after her as if she were a small baby yet she was now a child, healthy and growing. We could provide all the care she needed but it was physically very tiring. In addition, there were two other small children who also needed our physical presence and our loving parenting. There wasn't any spare energy to think about the future. I had decided that I would just take each day as it came and that was all I could do.

I didn't talk to many people about Sonia. It wasn't just that I didn't have the language, the society surrounding me didn't have it either. My parents and parents-in-law had been happy to look after her when she was small, but now it was physically too difficult for them. They felt helpless and didn't know what to do. We none of us ever discussed the situation;

no one talked about their feelings. Our parents were the generation who had lived through the war, resilient and able to cope with great hardship. They were not used to expressing their emotions or to enquiring about anyone else's. They just got on with their lives and expected everyone around them to do the same. They showed their love and concern in different ways. My mother would spend hours in shops buying pretty dresses and cardigans for Sonia, and my parents-in-law would always offer to babysit, as they lived nearer. We knew they all loved her so much – Sonia has always had the most appealing smile and infectious laughter – but they had no language to comfort us or themselves.

Our friends and local acquaintances were often awkward, not sure what to say or what not to say. If they saw us out and about with Sonia, who would sometimes be making her usual sounds, they looked worried that they might upset us if they said the wrong thing. People would stumble over their words, often beginning a sentence with, "I hope you don't mind my asking, but how is Sonia?" To which I would reply, "Of course I don't mind you asking. She's my daughter. I'm always happy to talk about her."

A lot of my emotional energy went into managing other people's feelings around Sonia. There wasn't anyone to help me manage mine and, in any event, I hadn't recognized that I needed any help or support of that kind. Brian and I were always kind to one another around her. Occasionally, I would wake in the night and find myself crying uncontrollably. I didn't feel alone as I knew Brian was sad too and he would do his best to comfort me. I promised myself that one day, when I had time, I would have a really good cry about the situation. But for now, there was too much else to think about.

TEN

FIVE YEARS OLD

One day, just before a trip to New York, my accountant rang to congratulate me. It must have been around our fourth or fifth year of trading, and he had just finished auditing the figures. Piatkus Books had achieved a turnover of £1,000,000 with a satisfactory profit. I hadn't set myself any financial targets and I remember that when he congratulated me it was quite a surprise. It was a wonderful milestone that I hadn't even noticed we'd reached, and I realized that I could afford to feel proud of myself for a few days and walk into American publishers' offices with a heightened feeling of confidence. In New York, I splurged on a beautiful Swiss watch to mark the occasion. I had never bought myself anything so expensive before. It was good value, though, as I am still wearing it to this day. It has always felt like a lucky talisman.

Every trip to New York was exciting. During each visit I would work (although it didn't feel like work) to build relationships with people who understood what Piatkus was trying to do and who were offering us books that they thought we would like to publish. Over the years, that grew to be a huge pleasure. In the 1980s, both American and British publishers wined and dined a lot; expense accounts were generous. On my trips to the States I would always choose to stay in a good hotel. One thing I had decided early on was that I was never going to play the "small publisher" card. I didn't want to keep reminding people that we were small and needed favours. I wanted to look as if we were doing well – indeed we were in our own way. It didn't matter that we were working from my home, we published books of a high standard and we were beginning to sell good quantities of some of them.

On reflection now, I probably also pursued that strategy because I was a woman. I wanted to behave as if I were a successful executive – even though I was watching like a hawk every dollar and cent I was spending. I was convinced (rightly or wrongly) that successful executives wouldn't have whinged about being "small". At the same time, the last thing I ever wanted to do was behave like a man. There were lots of advantages to being a woman in publishing as so many women work in the industry; I wanted everyone we dealt with to think of us as professional and reliable and doing well, so that they would know their books, if we bought them, would be in good hands.

I always offered to pay for meals and drinks on my trips, even though most publishers wouldn't let me (so I treated them when they came to London). I would start the day with breakfast either at my hotel or at a restaurant with one of my clients. Then I would visit one of the large companies and meet a couple of editors from different imprints in their huge skyscraper office block. The editors I met would tell me which new books they had bought for their list that they were excited about. I would speak with the directors who licensed foreign rights – which included England – and would go through their new book programmes while I told them what I wanted to consider for Piatkus. I was frequently invited to lunch in a trendy restaurant and then I would visit more people in their offices in the afternoon, before returning to the hotel to have drinks with a literary agent or an author.

If I had any spare time in this hectic schedule – a cancellation or a time slot I couldn't fill – I would head to the nearest bookshop. I always made time to roam the shelves and study the titles in the areas we were publishing. There were so many wonderful bookshops in New York before the internet took over

– so many branches of Barnes & Noble and Borders and unique stores such as Doubleday on Fifth Avenue. I loved my American trips and always returned home feeling very tired but happy and energized. It is so important to meet people in your own line of work, no matter what industry you are in. You learn from each other and see what you are trying to achieve from different points of view, which opens your mind to new understanding and ways of thinking. You become more creative.

After a while, I became very familiar with all the books in our chosen fields. Far fewer books were published in the 1980s and it was much easier to be aware of the competition for any new title. I realized early on that to make a name for ourselves in a publishing arena that was steadily becoming more competitive, we were going to have to continue to be trend-setters. We would have to be the ones taking risks and trying out new ideas. We couldn't sit at our desks waiting for people to offer us interesting new books, especially if that only meant we chased our tails in auctions where we would lose to conglomerates with more cash in their pockets. We had to be out there continually reminding agents and foreign publishers of our existence and our flair for innovation. We had to be visible. Not that anyone was using the term "visible" in the 1980s.

We were innovative but we also learned from the way our rivals published their books: from the covers they chose, the price points and even the formats. Every publishing company will have a different way of approaching the publication of the same book. When more than one publisher has made an offer for a book, an author will often decide which company to go to, based on the way they propose to publish the book.

I learned early on to ask my colleagues back home not to contact me while I was away. I didn't want to be thinking about anything that was happening in the office unless it was very important. I knew that in in my haste to make quick decisions and appear efficient, I could easily make small misjudgements. Portable computers did not exist then and information from the office would come to a foreign hotel by telex machine, fax or phone call. Every aspect of business moved much more slowly before email and it made for a much less stressful working day, whichever country you were based in. But making decisions about everyday matters is always harder when you are away from your normal routine, because your mind is filled with so much else to think about. Much better to deal with routine matters a week later when I was sitting at my desk and felt centred.

ELEVEN

CYRIL

It was 1984 and my marriage was at an end. It took me three days to pluck up the courage, and when I called my parents to tell them that Brian and I were no longer a couple, my mother said, "I'd always hoped you would divorce before you had children." She and my father had never thought we were suited. "You have too much ambition," they had said to me. Before we got married I hadn't really understood what they'd meant. Afterwards, I had thought we were sufficiently well matched that it wouldn't matter. I thought I had so much ambition that it would be enough for both of us. But sadly it did matter. Twelve years previously, an intellectually brilliant, somewhat eccentric young man had married a young girl who had not yet been shaped by the world. Now I had become a very different woman from the shy eighteen-year-old I had been when we first met.

For many years, as a teenager and into my early twenties, I had very low self-esteem and if you had asked me to describe myself, I would have said I was "a mousy secretary". Outwardly confident, only I knew how difficult I sometimes found it to speak up about what was important to me. While I was able to be assertive when I needed to be on behalf of my company, I hated conflict in my personal life and would do whatever I could to try to avoid it. Like many young women brought up to please, I had never been good at understanding or handling my own anger, which was often deeply buried. It was not until several years later – and then some – that I really felt comfortable in my own skin.

As I found myself thrust into the position of having to earn a good living, the latent ambition rising in me had begun to rock our marriage (as my parents had shrewdly foreseen). My publishing company was becoming well known and, as that rare object, a woman in business, I was receiving regular calls to be featured in the media. I felt it made my husband uncomfortable and a huge gap grew between us. It gradually became obvious that it wouldn't be possible for us to find a way to bridge it together.

Many couples are unable to live together after the birth of a child with disabilities. Yet I never thought Sonia was the cause of our marriage ending. We were always very kind and gentle with one another around her. We both recognized the grief that was always held in check, and we both always wanted the best for her. My husband was a loving father who adored his children.

I felt it would be better if I moved out of the family home for a while. In the early 1980s, the breakup of a family was not always widely supported or approved of; although, with more women entering the workplace and contributing to the family income, that attitude was gradually changing. I went to see a solicitor to ask about my legal position before I moved out. He looked at me patronizingly and said, "It's just a phase. You'll get over it. I advise you to go back home and give it another try."

Sometimes I have thought that if I had been given £10 as an apology for every middle-aged man who has patronized me in my life, I would have been a multi-millionaire before I was in my forties. But I wasn't so feisty then and didn't answer back. I simply found another solicitor – a woman this time – who came highly recommended. And so I moved on. And after a few months, the children came to live with me and my husband and I set up a visitation system that worked for many years. Nevertheless, our divorce was acrimonious and our continuing relationship over the years has always been very difficult.

I once met a woman who spoke about how she had stayed in her unhappy marriage for many years until she found the courage to leave her husband. In the months afterwards she had prayed constantly, sending love to him and to her daughter and to the relationship between them. She managed to continue doing this for a long time and eventually she was able to heal the rift between them. I don't know if I could have managed that but, certainly, no one suggested it to me back then. I had become unhappy in the marriage and my sadness had permeated everything during the last few years we shared as a family while we struggled to achieve some level of happiness. Now I was free. I had no regrets because my grieving for our relationship had happened while we were together. I had some savings and interesting work and I could afford a nanny who would also babysit. I resolved that I was going to be happy from now on.

I moved out of our home into a rented house in Princes Road in Buckhurst Hill, a pretty suburb on the edge of Epping Forest and just down the road from the family home in Loughton. It was unlike anywhere I had lived before: an old Edwardian house, not yet restored. The lounge and kitchen were on the ground floor and behind the kitchen was the bathroom. When I first moved in, it was possible to see through the window pane on the front door and along the hall passage into the kitchen. It felt very strange creeping downstairs at night to have a bath, until I had the bright idea of fixing a towel across the pane of glass so that no one outside could see through. Not that I was expecting many visitors. People who knew us as a family were all shocked by the situation. Overnight, I had become a pariah in some circles; yet other friends were supportive, recognizing the hopelessness of the situation and also seeing no future for us together. I was very grateful to all those people.

After a while, I felt ready to embark on a new social life. I didn't want to visit the friends we had made as a couple and sit at their tables, spilling out the sorry story. I had been single in my early twenties and now I was going to be single in my thirties, albeit now an entrepreneur and a mother. But I wasn't planning to get married again for a long, long time, if ever.

Because I had a live-in nanny to babysit, I was able to go out in the evening sometimes after the children were in bed. In addition, they spent alternate weekends with their father, who was still living in the house in Loughton. One day, my friend Jo, who had been divorced a couple of years longer than me, invited me to a party organized by a singles group. I remember what I wore that night. In the 1980s, there were so few women in senior positions in business that there was no uniform. It was a colourful era and I worked in the media. Twice a year I would go and buy a few designer clothes – they were more affordable then – and I would wear one item each day of the week for work. The night of the party I was wearing my favourite outfit, a red woollen Escada jumper with a dainty black flower appliqued onto the front, and I wore it with a matching red pleated skirt. I always felt good in it with my glossy long black boots. It was such a wonderful period for fabulous clothes. A few years later, all that changed; after the recession of the 1990s, women entering the workplace in senior positions all felt obliged to dress like men, in dark suits of grey, navy or black. Gone was the vivacity of the decade before; in the sombre recession we dressed to look suitable and definitely not to draw attention to our femininity.

I don't remember much about the party except that I danced – my husband had hated to dance – and felt confident in my singleness. After all, everyone here was single, although some of them hadn't been married yet. I decided to go to another of these events a short while later. This time, Jo couldn't come with me so I walked into the room alone. It was something I was getting used to – the letting go of physical coupledom, something people feel particularly aware of after a separation. On that night I was wearing another favourite outfit, a one-piece with black culottes trimmed with gold, with a sassy matching gold and black belt – and my favourite black boots of course. I paused in the doorway and looked around the room. I didn't know anyone. I saw an attractive, dark-haired, Italian-looking man in a beige and brown jumper sitting opposite the door. *He looks interesting*, I thought. *I'll go and sit next to him.*

We talked for three hours. I was finding my way in this new world of single and divorced men, realizing that I liked to make up my own mind about people without them knowing too much about me too quickly. I never spoke about my ex-husband or my family, and when men asked whether I worked for a living and what I did, I would say, "I work in publishing", and if they wanted to know more, I would say, "We publish romantic novels." Titillating, true and yet not quite the whole story.

The man in the beige and brown jumper was interested in what I had to say. He too was an entrepreneur and we had much in common. I was enjoying myself, though also a little nervous. Aside from my work colleagues, I hadn't spent this long talking to another man in a social situation, just the two of us, for many years. There was a bowl of peanuts on a table beside us and gradually I worked my way through the whole lot. When the event came to an end, my companion went off to speak to the hostess. *He hasn't asked for my number*, I thought. *Well, if he doesn't want it, I'm not waiting around.* I got my coat and left the house.

My car was parked nearby and, as I was about to drive away, the front door of the house opened and suddenly someone was running down the road, waving at the car. "Will you have dinner with me on Saturday night?" he asked.

It wasn't a straightforward romance and we did see other people for a while, but six months later it had become just the two of us; and two and a half years later we began to live together. Now, as I write this, the conversation between Cyril and myself has lasted a long time, day and night, for the last thirty-five years.

Fortunately, or perhaps wisely, in this new relationship I had found a man who recognized my intrinsic need to use my brain in the workplace. In 1986, a book was published, *The Business Amazons*, written by Leah Hertz. She had originally wanted to interview businesswomen who owned the controlling shares in their companies, had a turnover of more than one million pounds and a staff of more than twenty. She could not find fifty women in the UK who fitted that criteria so she backtracked a little and chose not to worry about the number of staff. *The Business Amazons* was the first study of women business owners and was a reminder of how few of us there were with sizeable businesses at that time. Leah quotes me – though not by my real name – as saying that I liked selling things and I didn't like housework and that, if I had not made a success of my business, it would have been very hard for my family because I would not have been a happy wife and mother. Luckily, Cyril has always admired and supported me, acknowledged my achievements and encouraged me to give of my best. He has unstintingly given of his best to be there for me. Building my company and stepping bravely forward into the future with Cyril by my side has turned out to be the very best thing that could ever have happened.

TWELVE
FOLLOW THE MONEY

The Piatkus Books office and employees had moved out of the Loughton house at the end of 1983. We didn't know where our journey would end, but it was time to move on to the next stage of our growth. We had heard about a small office in Hanway Street, close to Oxford Circus, which had been rented by Gill's husband's company and was no longer needed by them. We took it on temporarily.

From the quiet streets of Loughton we were now in the bustling West End. The energy was powerful, pulsating through us. It was a huge change from the much slower pace of life in the loft.

Our stay wasn't going to be permanent because the little office, in a narrow building beside a dubious pub, wasn't large enough to allow for expansion. Nevertheless, it gave us a pause so we could plan for what would come next. We were on the second, third and fourth floors, and at various times of day we would come down the narrow, rickety stairs to find a gaping hole had opened at the bottom – into which the bar staff would be unloading their latest deliveries through a trapdoor. The pub's most popular dish on the menu must have been macaroni cheese or Welsh rarebit as the building perpetually smelt of burnt cheese.

June had decided she didn't want to continue working for us because she didn't want to commute into town, though she promised to come and help out if we ever desperately needed her. We were going to miss her; older than all of us, we often relied on her wisdom and common sense. Very sadly she had a sudden heart attack and passed away just a few months later, still only in her early fifties. She was the first friend of mine who had died and I felt her loss very deeply. Her passing cast a shadow over all of us, thinking of her every time we came across her handwriting and notes in the files while we settled into our new routines.

Dorothy and Jane enjoyed working in the West End and all of us were delighted to be joined by Doreen, who had been our cleaning lady in Loughton before having her hours augmented by becoming our postmistress. She went to classes to learn typing and joined us in town as our full-time receptionist and typist. Several years later she got a better paid job working in the City. I always admired her commitment and hard work.

We celebrated the fifth birthday of the company in 1984 with a special cocktail party in a trendy London venue, Peppermint Park. Book publishing is an industry which, more than many others, is all about relationships and hype. For a small company we had already achieved many successes. We wanted to achieve many more and our guests were the people who had enabled us to achieve this milestone and would hopefully continue to support us in the future. We invited all the people who had helped us to reach that pivotal moment – authors, booksellers, literary agents and many more. Publishing is all about celebrations and each new book published by a small company is always a unique endeavour and a labour of love.

Ensconced in our new town office, our staff gradually began to increase. Mac was one of our next hires, a man in his sixties, an experienced bookkeeper who had recently retired from his job at a well-known building firm. He would come into the office two days a week. Another young woman, Helen, joined as the first full-time member of our production team. The production of books – the actual making of them – is a key department in every publishing house. Until that time, I had been producing the fiction, which was not difficult as all our books were the same non-illustrated format and were reprints or hardbacks of books that were coming out in paperback, which had already been set and designed by the original publisher. All we had to do was change the first few pages of the book, known as prelims, insert our logo and company details and submit it to our printers.

A freelance team had been producing our non-fiction and the relationship was working well. Now we needed someone in-house to manage all the fiction, the cover artwork (which had been created for us by freelance designers) and our increasing need for reprints. Our books were increasingly being considered for sale alongside those of the larger publishing houses and we felt we needed to up our game and achieve a greater level of sophistication with our cover designs. Now Gill and I needed to delegate the organization of the printing processes so that we could free ourselves to do what each of us did best – to run the company in my case, and to edit in hers. She continued to work from home, as did Jana for a good part of the time. On the top floor of the new office, there was a tiny room under the eaves where there was just enough space for Philip and me to have a desk each. This would be our first time working opposite each other. All of us were excited by the new office setup. But we knew it couldn't last long if we were to grow.

My years of working from home had been the greatest blessing financially. I had managed to build up precious capital by having so few employees in the first couple of years and then by putting in the loft extension and not having to pay rent. Now that we had moved out of the Loughton house, my safety net was starting to fall away. I had rental commitments and the wages bill was increasing fast. I was going to have to pay much more attention to the finances, I realized. We would have to be careful not to run out of money.

In the 1980s, it was possible to receive enough orders in advance of the print run for it to be paid for before the books were produced. The challenge was to get enough books sold and get the money in before we had to pay the printer and cover the overheads each month. General publishing is a labour-intensive activity and the price of every book is very low considering the huge amount of work that goes into making it. Time spent reading and selecting titles to publish; commissioning of new books based on a full synopsis; structural editing of a typescript when it is delivered; copyediting and proofreading; picture selection (if required); design of book and cover – and that is all before the book is ready to go to the production department. Meanwhile, there's the work of the sales department, persuading customers all over the world to place advance orders and the material written and produced to help them do so. It was straightforward to understand; it wasn't so easy to achieve.

We were not planning to produce highly illustrated books. I have always been naturally independent and at that time illustrated books entailed working with a co-edition partner to create a print run large enough to cover the great expense of producing them. If we had a good idea for a book I wanted to be able to go it alone. Many publishers, including Dorling Kindersley, Hamlyn and Octopus, were creating beautiful illustrated books and I had no inclination to compete in that market. What I was looking for were books that we could produce fairly simply, mainly in black-and-white text, which would go on to sell thousands of copies.

Most published books sell very few copies. It isn't always possible to know in advance the quality of the book the author will deliver, and some subjects that sound interesting at an early stage will have been published by other houses before you can get your book out. Even the largest and most successful publishing houses frequently make mistakes. It is always easy to publish books but not so easy to produce books that keep reprinting. Finding those elusive titles is a thrill, and many publishers have lost their companies and homes by printing too many copies of books no one wanted to buy. On a trip to Las Vegas, wanting to experience a casino for the first time, I decided to allow myself a budget of $50 to play. I began to slip coins into some of the machines and, after about ten minutes, I realized that this was child's play compared to what I was getting up to in the office every day. Using our combined expertise, we were regularly betting thousands of pounds on projects that might or might not make their money back. In Las Vegas, I had soon had enough; at Piatkus, the thrill of the game carried on.

Our contract for the office in Hanway Street was very flexible, but after a few months it became clear that we would soon need to move offices again. We were already using every inch of space. I began to dream of owning our own building, a space that belonged solely to us, where no one could continually raise the rent or tell us what to do. This was all happening at the time my marriage broke up. First, I needed to find a place for the three children and me to live; then I would sort out the office situation.

I was climbing the ladder of success but there was no one holding it steady at the bottom. I needed to change that and find a way to feel secure.

THIRTEEN
NEW ROOTS

North London was to be my next destination, nearer my family and several friends, and I wanted to move there before the September school term began, especially so I could get my son Matthew settled. He had already started school in Essex and there was enough disruption in his life with which to contend. I began to view houses and, after just a couple of weeks, came upon the perfect home in Totteridge. It was in the catchment area of the new school I wanted the younger children to attend and was near Woodside Park tube station to take me into town; it had four bedrooms and a bright, sunny aspect and every room had fitted wardrobes. Even more extraordinary, the owner had just emigrated and had left behind some furniture. It was just what we needed in every way.

I had been squirreling my salary away for some time and was able to obtain a mortgage for three times my salary. In those days, getting a mortgage was a very quick process and the children, their nanny and I were able to move in within a few weeks of making the offer for the house, just before the school term began. I found a little nursery for Leah, who was the first child to be settled, and Sonia was soon offered a place at a suitable school that had a good reputation. A minibus would pick her up quite early each morning and bring her home in the afternoon. This was a wonderful arrangement for us. We felt so grateful. Gradually Matthew was found a place at the local primary I wanted for him and my everyday life became much calmer.

I had only met Cyril a few months previously and we weren't to live together for another couple of years. A succession of nannies came to live with us, many from Australia and New Zealand. We could never tell which ones would stay a year or more, or who would leave after just a few months – they never knew themselves – but somehow the household managed to keep afloat. I was very grateful that running my own company enabled me to manage my own time. If I had to leave late for work or go home early to meet Sonia's school bus because the nanny couldn't do it for any reason, I could adjust my diary accordingly. In fact, things tended to run smoothly and it didn't happen very often that I had to rush home unexpectedly in the middle of the day. I was lucky enough to have healthy children who didn't need to be home from school very much.

Meanwhile, I was falling in love with Cyril and we were spending a lot of time together and especially enjoying the alternate weekends when the children were staying with their father. There were times when I felt completely swept off my feet. Reading two or three romantic novels a week was part of my work and now I couldn't believe my luck and good fortune. Here was a partner who was always saying lovely things to me and I sensed he was completely genuine. It never bothered him that I had three small children; he was always very loving towards Sonia, comfortably pushing her wheelchair through the streets and to the park, just happy to be with all of us. He met me at the point in my life where I had blossomed in confidence, comfortable with the triple role of being a happy woman, loving mother and professional business owner. I never had to hide any parts of myself from him. We met as equals in our private lives and in the business world – and that suited both of us. Our values were similar in so many ways and there was always so much to share. We were thrilled to have found one another.

When Sonia was very young, I had put her name on a waiting list to go to live in Ravenswood Village, now run by an organization called Norwood, a unique place situated in beautiful wooded countryside near Crowthorne in Berkshire. It had been established in the 1950s, when a group of parents came together to create a home for their disabled children where they would be lovingly cared for after the parents had died. At this time, it was a home for around 150 residents who lived together in small units, looked after by carers. Ambulant residents were able to wander freely and safely around the village, and there was a special school for children up to the age of eighteen. The underlying ethos of the organization was to offer the people who lived there the best possible quality of life that they would be able to experience.

I'd had it in mind that it would be a good place for Sonia to live one day and I had been in touch with the organization when she was very young. I was hoping that by the time she reached eighteen and left school, there might be the possibility of her living there as an adult. But there was no guarantee that the opportunity would ever be available for her when she was older, because there was fierce competition and she needed such a high level of care. However, when Sonia was nine, I received a call asking if I was still interested in a place for her at the Village as there was one available. Sonia could go to school there and she would live with children her own age.

The caller seemed especially empathetic because I was a single mother and things were not always easy for the four of us. I was hesitant. Sonia was still so young. But when I was assured that there would be a long procedure to go through to get funding, and she might not be suitable anyway, I thought I would go ahead and fill in the forms, and meet the various social workers. I was aware that the North London house where we were living would not be suitable for her long term. There was a short flight of steps up to the front door (something I had not taken into consideration when I had bought it so hastily). Every time we all went out, I either had to carry Sonia up and down the front steps before manipulating her into a car seat, or we had to lift the wheelchair through the garden door with Sonia in it, and wheel her out the back gate and down the shared drive beside the house. There was no downstairs loo; morning and evening, either the nanny or I would carry her up and down the stairs, usually fireman's lift style. I thought I would be able to carry on doing this for a while yet. But not indefinitely as Sonia was getting taller and heavier.

Now I look back and I am much older, it seems odd that I didn't worry about Sonia's future. But I know that I didn't partly due to my temperament. I am not by nature a worrier; I am a problem-solver. Sonia was my daughter and I loved her so much that it never occurred to me that we wouldn't find a way to get through life together. When we needed to, we would move into a more convenient house. I always had so much to think about on a daily basis that there wasn't space to worry about problems that might not arise for a few years. I wasn't expecting to consider Sonia's future adult life until she was ready to leave school.

After the various assessments, a letter arrived a few months later informing me that there was a place for Sonia at Ravenswood Village and asking whether I would like to accept it. I was hesitant, but a decision had to be made. Sonia was part of our family unit, yet I thought that if I did not accept the place on her behalf, there might not be another chance when she was older. With a heavy heart, I accepted the place. I knew I was giving her the best opportunity of a life where she would always be cared for and where she would have the chance to experience the best that she was capable of enjoying. But it was so hard to let her go at the age of nine – even though she would be able to come home for weekends on a coach, travelling with other residents. A wise friend said to me, "If Sonia were going to university, you would have to let her go when she was eighteen. So it's really just happening a few years earlier."

The day the children and I took Sonia and her favourite toys, clothes and possessions to the Village, we were welcomed warmly. It was all very informal. Sonia would sleep in her own pretty bedroom with a large window looking out onto woodland. There was another little girl her own age who had recently arrived, and they would go to school together – the school building was just a few steps away – and enjoy swimming in the indoor pool. All the facilities were suitable for wheelchairs. The residents would be cared for by trained carers who had chosen to work there. The quality of Sonia's daily experience would be far better in so many ways than we had been or would ever be able to offer.

Gradually Sonia settled in and, to everyone's delight, she began to thrive. It turned out that she was much better at getting her needs met in the Village than she had been at home. In our family home, she couldn't always have what she wanted when she wanted it because there was also her brother and sister to consider. There were times when her siblings' ability to run around and do things she couldn't irritated and frustrated her very much. In the Village, where all the residents were more equal, Sonia's powerful presence soon established her as queen bee and very soon everyone was eating out of her hand. She was meeting friendly new people who knew how to be with her and who made a fuss of her all the time.

For a long time after Sonia went to live in the Village, I felt like I had lost a limb. There was an invisible part of me that wasn't there anymore. I had let her go so she could have a better life, and it was a deep and strange kind of loss. Until she left us, I hadn't allowed myself to reflect on my feelings about her and our years spent at home together. I had never allowed myself – or had time – to properly grieve for the difficulties in her life and all the challenges for us as a family. When she was small I had understood how powerful my feelings of loss were, that she wasn't growing up to be the child all parents are hoping for – the "normal" child. But her personal struggle to get through each day was such a mountainous, all-encompassing one that it dwarfed all of my own painful feelings. While I had intimate knowledge of the loss of my own hopes and dreams, I could not begin to imagine what it must be like to be Sonia, unable to express her wants and needs effortlessly. I also had no understanding that there might even be anything that I needed to "deal with" emotionally. Naturally, I thought about Sonia every day and when I talked about her, or answered people's questions, after a few moments I would always feel a lump come into the back of my throat so that I could hardly carry on speaking. I missed her so much.

With only the two younger children, now aged seven and five, in the house, our daily lives became much easier. We began to receive more invitations because people had hesitated to invite us to visit as a family when Sonia was at home. We had the freedom to go out when we wanted; we could simply put our coats on and walk out the front door. We no longer had to plan for wheelchair access, which was hard to do in the 1980s when the rights of the disabled was a virtually unknown concept.

Living with Sonia had been a struggle because communication was so difficult. We had to guess what her needs were all the time, to work our way through a list of alternatives, just as with a young baby or toddler. Hunger, thirst, too hot or cold, inside, outside, pain, nappy change, too loud or quiet, different music. (Sonia loved music but, like all of us, could suddenly tire of what she was listening to and want something different played – but of course she couldn't tell us what her preference was.) The younger children and I had done our best to make her happy and had coped with the situation as best we could.

In the first few years after Sonia moved to the Village, she came home regularly for weekends and we went often to visit her. There was a special softball playroom in her unit – a novelty for all of us, as all the children could play in it at the same time. There were often squeals of laughter, and it was lovely to see them able to enjoy an activity together. We could walk around the surrounding wooded area or go for a short drive in the car. After a while people in the local towns of Crowthorne or Bracknell would stop us when they saw us coming, introducing themselves and saying hello to Sonia. Many of them worked in the Village or had members of their family who did. Sonia's community of friends was growing and she was happily settling in to her new life.

A few months after Sonia went to live in the Village, Cyril moved in to live with us. His teenage daughter, still at school, would continue to live with his ex-wife and visit in the holidays. I remember clearing out a wardrobe and drawers for him; I hoped he wasn't going to bring too much luggage. I wondered what kind of possessions he owned. It felt very strange at this time in my life – almost like a flat-share, except I hadn't done that since I was twenty-one. Cyril's arrival felt very formal as we both worked politely to accommodate each other's needs and wishes. The children took it all in their stride as they had become used to Cyril visiting at weekends. I looked forward to the time when we would have established a routine as a household and everything would feel more relaxed.

My parents were a little wary at first, not knowing what to make of Cyril, who was completely different from my previous husband or any of the young men who they had known when I was growing up. Gradually, though, they began to warm to him as they could see how lovingly he cared for all of us.

FOURTEEN

WINDMILL STREET

Now that the family was settled in Totteridge, it was time to turn my attention to finding an office building. This decision, made at such an early stage in the life of the company, was the most important one we took around that time as it allowed Piatkus Books to stay independent over the next twenty years.

Buying an office building might not be the best decision for every start-up. I knew that if the company owned a bricks-and-mortar asset, the bank would be comfortable lending us money and would not suddenly ring us up and demand repayment of any overdraft that was not supported by some kind of guarantee. For us, it was the catalyst in enabling us to prosper. At the same time, owning the building enabled me to sleep soundly at night. Because we had been careful with money in the early years, we had built up some capital. Now I needed a mortgage.

I had not always had good experiences with bank managers. In 1981, after Piatkus Books had been trading for two financial years and I was on my way to a turnover of a quarter of a million pounds, I'd decided to apply for an overdraft. Our customers were mainly libraries at that time, reliable state-funded organizations, and after two years of trading I could already show growth and consistency in our earnings. My accountant helped me draw up a cash flow statement and I made an appointment to see the manager of the local bank where Brian and I had had a joint personal account. He heard my story – how I had already sold one business, made some money and was using the capital for the new enterprise – and reviewed our figures. It was clear from our bank statements that money was flowing in to the business account that was in my name only. In spite of that, at the end of the meeting he had said, "I will be happy to give you an overdraft as long as your husband co-signs as a guarantor." I was shocked. Even when I told him that my husband wasn't involved with the business, he refused to change his attitude. I was a married woman with small children. I could not have an overdraft on my own. At the time, I had called my accountant for advice and he had recommended another bank manager, who was perfectly happy to give me an overdraft after he had examined the figures. He understood the business and how it worked and he could see we knew what we were doing.

A few years had passed since then. Now, with a turnover of upwards of a million, getting an increased overdraft and a mortgage was much easier. Over a period of several years, staying disciplined and taking the minimum amount of money out of the company in salary, I had been able to build up enough money in the company for the mortgage deposit. Not since the £500 my father had given me to jointly set up Severn House had anyone given me any money.

Along the way, I had had to give up the family home and start again. It had been an amazing rollercoaster ride, and now I was going to be personally responsible both for the mortgage on my house and one on an office building. I made a vow that the two would never be interlinked. I took a lot of risks but I would never have gambled the roof over my children's heads.

We had found a small freehold building of about 2,800 square feet in Windmill Street, a little road just off London's popular Charlotte Street. The price was £115,000 and we took out a mortgage with payments roughly equivalent to what we would be paying if we were renting. The difference was that the rent on space in a Central London office building would likely have gone up. We had fifteen years to try to pay off the outstanding sum.

The building had lots of daylight. We had three floors of space with windows back and front on most floors. There was also a sizeable basement for storage, with room for a parcel-packing bench. In the days before digital, we liked to keep a lot of our books on site and we were always posting copies of typescripts, proofs and finished books to authors, customers, reviewers and suppliers. We would later employ someone simply to pack all our post every day.

The day we moved in was so exciting. There was so much empty space. We purchased desks, bookshelves and filing cabinets. Everyone had plenty of room to make themselves at home – and people did, bringing in photos, spider plants and ferns, favourite mugs and other bits and pieces with which to surround themselves. Each floor was open plan but no two desk spaces were alike. There were some fitted cupboards in the room on the third floor, which were suitable for storing typescripts, and I bought three solid teak bookcases in the sale at Heal's furniture store in Tottenham Court Road for display purposes. After our time working in the tiny little loft room in Hanway Street, Philip and I were used to, and enjoyed, working in the same space. We agreed to share the third-floor office and divided it with a glass partition containing a blind so we could have privacy if either of us wanted it. But most of the time we left the door open and shouted across the room to one another or stood in the doorway to have a conversation. Over the years, there was very little about the company that we didn't share and discuss together: thoughts and ideas, trade gossip, strategy and intelligence.

All the staff were so proud of our office, feeling that owning our own building was a huge achievement for all our efforts so far. It gave us enormous credibility, especially when we wanted to make the point that we were not some fly-by-night organization, which was necessary sometimes with new authors and others in the publishing trade who needed to be reassured that we were sufficiently experienced and reliable.

When we first moved into Windmill Street, we considered the possibility of renting out some of the space as there were only eight of us at that time, but it wasn't long before we realized that we would be needing it for ourselves. Our next key hire was our production manager, Simon Colverson, who had worked for several publishing companies and was of similar age to me. My colleagues and I had enjoyed working with the freelance team who produced our non-fiction, but now we realized it was time for our production to be managed in-house. Taking on a new and senior member of staff is always an important step for a relatively small organization. Having Simon join us was a sign that we were building a serious business that was beginning to increase significantly in achievement and value.

There had unexpectedly been some mild interest in buying the company and I was therefore interested in discovering what we were worth. I learned that general publishing companies, as opposed to academic or educational ones, were valued according to turnover. As a general rule, at that time, if one's turnover was one million pounds, then the company would be worth approximately that sum minus outstanding debts. I kept this in mind as we grew. If we got into trouble financially, I always had in the back of my mind what we would be worth. I was a single mother with three young children, one of whom would likely never be able to walk. It was a lot of responsibility.

The value of a publishing company is also calculated in terms of its intellectual property, namely how strongly books in its backlist continue to perform. A strong backlist is the Holy Grail of the industry. By 1985, when we moved into Windmill Street, we were continuing to publish four novels every month. Most of these had a short lifespan. However, the number of titles we were publishing by our handful of bestselling novelists was increasing and we were often required to produce new editions of those. At the same time, we were expanding our non-fiction list and our strategy with those books was to create titles that would hopefully have much longer lives. Publishing is a high-risk activity and expensive mistakes are common. Publishers can pay too high an advance for a title or waste a huge amount of money getting the print run wrong. Legendary stories abound in the industry of massive advances paid to authors whose books only sell a few copies. No rivals can afford to gloat, because every publishing house knows how easy it is to get carried away with the excitement of an auction, making a generous offer for a book that turns out to be a complete dud. With every new book, money goes out and it is often a couple of years before you see a return on your investment. During those times, the stronger the backlist of books that sell all the time, the more able a publisher is to finance the current programme and invest in future books.

There was one problem in creating good non-fiction backlist titles that I had not foreseen and which began to impact on us soon after we moved into Windmill Street. When we reprinted a novel by Danielle Steel, for example, the cost of the reprint was not very high. But a reprint of *Fast Cakes* was much more expensive because we had to print many more copies of our larger-format illustrated books to make the costs work. I became used to constantly juggling in my head how many copies of books we could afford to reprint in any one month, calculating how each reprint would impact on cash flow.

The printers usually invoiced us at the end of each month, and we learned quickly to cheekily manipulate delivery dates for the reprints to come at the beginning of each month so that we would have an extra few weeks' credit. Fortunately the printers were happy to work in partnership, as they could see that we were producing books that sold well and the reprint orders were coming thick and fast. All of them were hugely supportive, most of them refraining from giving us too hard a time when we were slow to pay our invoices. I always appreciated that they didn't chase us for money as hard as they might have done. At the same time, we always did our best to tell them the truth about when we would be able to pay them. If we said we would pay them in a week's time, we did our very best to stick to it.

We bought Simon a large desk and he established himself in a corner space on the second floor. He was responsible for all our printing requirements – books, covers, brochures, every kind of illustrated material. We had already employed a manager who handled our fiction production. Now we had a whole department (of two) and all our records would be rigorously accurate.

When we sold the company many years later, Simon was still in his position in the corner office. He had become a director of the company by then – well known and respected by everyone in the book trade – and his tiny production department (impressively still only two people) had been responsible for producing nearly three thousand books and thousands of reprints. Over the years, we had had only a very few occasions when a book had not been delivered to the warehouse on time, and even delayed books were only late by a very few days. We had been so lucky that Simon had made the decision in 1986 to work in our young enterprise.

FIFTEEN
MOVING FORWARDS

In the first years of our business, we were experimenting with different genres and finding out what we were good at. Often the books we published were about subjects that either Gill or I were familiar with or interested to learn more about. It was an office joke that you could see what was going on in my personal life by looking at the books we were publishing. *Mary Berry's Food Processor Cookbook* and *Mary Berry's Freezer Cookbook* were examples of books I wanted to own so that I could enjoy my Magimix at home more and learn to cook for the freezer.

One day, Philip came into the office, very excited about an organization called The Curry Club, which he had read about in that morning's newspaper. The Club had been founded by Pat Chapman who, in his spare time from his day job as a lighting engineer, had built up a number of groups throughout the UK to bring together people who enjoyed curry. His first book for Piatkus, *Curry Club Indian Restaurant Cookbook*, sold well and began to backlist, and when he suggested we published *Curry Club Balti Cookbook*, we took his advice although we didn't know what balti was. (In fact it is a particular type of curry cooked and served in a special dish.)

Word quickly began to spread about the new book. Jana did us proud with the publicity and a launch was organized for key buyers and journalists at a restaurant in Birmingham, where there were already many balti restaurants. It was therefore a huge thrill to open the *Sunday Times* the week after the launch and see the book listed there in the top five bestselling hardbacks. It was a proud and special moment for us. We continued to publish Curry Club titles for many years. The organization grew in size and Indian restaurants were proud to display the colourful Curry Club logo in their windows when we published the *Good Curry Guide*. Every time we published a new Curry Club cookbook, it enabled us to re-offer the backlist. It was a brilliant success for everyone involved.

Other areas in which Piatkus began to do well were those of parenting and popular psychology. In the UK, people had always been much slower to buy "how to" and self-help books than their compatriots abroad, but times were changing. When we did cautiously publish in the parenting and healthcare areas, we found that many of the books sold very well. Before the internet, if you didn't consult a professional in person, your only source of written reference information was from books. Readers bought or borrowed them from friends – or borrowed them from the library. Slowly, booksellers gave more space in the shops to parenting and healthcare titles. Piatkus's books on topics such as *Sleepless Children* by Dr David Haslam, *Feeding Your Children* by Miranda Hall, *Living with a Teenager* by Suzie Hayman and *Okay Parenting* by Mavis Klein found their niche markets both in bookshops and in the children's book clubs. All of them contributed to our growing backlist of solid reference books.

After my divorce, we also ventured into popular psychology, trying out a few American titles. Some of them, such as *How to Find Your Ideal Man* and *Adult Children of Divorce*, were reflective of my new status. Later came more American trends, including *Home Coming: Reclaiming and Championing Your Inner Child* by John Bradshaw and books on codependency. Again, the British market was cautious. They weren't quite ready for this influx of navel-gazing. That wasn't to happen until a few years later.

At the same time as building our non-fiction list of backlisting titles, we continued to build our reputation for publishing solid commercial fiction. Our backlist now included more bestselling novels by Danielle Steel, V. C. Andrews and Cynthia Freeman. We were only publishing hardback editions for libraries and book clubs, each book only generating a small profit, but because they didn't require much in-house time and because we would publish several titles every month, our fiction was a very good income stream.

During the decade we built up a reputation for being able to spot winners and this helped our lesser known books to sell alongside them. We published library hardbacks of early titles by Harlan Coben, Michael Palmer and an author called Leigh Nichols, who was actually one of the pseudonyms of the bestselling thriller-writer Dean Koontz. One of his titles, *The Eyes of Darkness*, which Piatkus originally published in hardback, became very well known in 2020 as many readers discussed whether the plot had predicted the COVID-19 pandemic. The success of these, and others, gave us confidence to begin to venture into our own original fiction publishing. We couldn't pay very high advances, but there were always a lot of authors on offer both in the UK and in America. We had to find the needles in the haystack who would make a profit for us, and we published a few first novels by authors who went on to have stellar careers, including Robert Crais, Peter May and Robert B. Parker.

In the middle of the decade, there had been a brief flutter of interest from the public in very steamy romances called "bodice-rippers". These originated in America and the covers usually showed a woman in wild disarray, accompanied by a supposedly sexy, long-haired man looking adoringly at her. We had done a deal with Corgi books to publish several of these titles in hardback for the libraries and they sold well. Luckily we didn't have to originate all the covers and were able to use the Corgi material. Our list included some of the global bestsellers in the genre, including Kathleen E. Woodiwiss and Johanna Lindsey. We found that women were often much more likely to take a chance and read a book by an author they had not heard of if they liked the cover and the idea behind the storyline.

We could sell many more books to women by unknown authors. In contrast, men, for the most part, prefer to buy known brands. It was therefore easier to experiment with building female authors than it was for us to build a thriller writer from scratch. The latter needed a substantial marketing budget and we couldn't afford it. Our fiction publishing rarely made huge profits, but its big advantage was that it was easy to produce and sold quickly. While it could take several months for our non-fiction books to earn their money back, our novels would usually break even on publication. It was good to have two such different streams of income. The constant flow of money coming in from our fiction could be easily estimated and relied upon, even though, throughout the decade, library funds from the government were slowly being cut and the quantity of books we could hope to sell to libraries was beginning to diminish. If we had a lean month with our non-fiction – and some calendar months are often very quiet for sales – then the regular fiction income would be very welcome to our cash flow.

All businesses, no matter their size, are about managing risk, staying alert, and watching the marketplace as it shifts and changes. We were answerable to no one in the strategies we pursued. But everyone in the building was always aware that their contribution made a difference. The 1980s was a very good decade for the company. We had established ourselves as a publisher to be taken seriously. We had created a strong range of books that continued to sell. Philip had built up the export side of our business. We were well placed, we thought, to enter the next decade. But then, as is common in all business ventures, the cycle turned. There had been several years of national economic growth but at the end of the decade a sudden downturn in the economy heralded a complete sea-change. Suddenly people stopped spending, sales slowed, the commercial world fell into recession. When we had launched the company at the beginning of the 1980s, times had been difficult, but our overheads were low and we hadn't known any other kind of trading environment. Now we had an office filled with staff who all had to be paid at the end of the month, alongside our mortgage and other commitments.

It was to be our first experience of running a business during times of hardship. Everything we had built and everything we were doing was suddenly called into question when the recession of the early 1990s hit. We were a tiny boat sailing on a massive sea, buffeted by winds of change that we had absolutely no control over. Did we have the courage and the ability to be flexible enough to survive?

SIXTEEN

RECESSION

The recession of the early 1990s was a sharp, painful wake-up call, a forerunner to the advent of globalization that was to completely change the way so many companies traded with one another, both at home and overseas.

In the boom of the 1980s, most ordinary people's financial situation had begun to improve after the economic gloom that had preceded it. Margaret Thatcher's rhetoric had encouraged people to become self-reliant entrepreneurs and go-getters, and to rely less on the state to provide for them. It was acceptable to be aspirational. In the middle of the decade we had published a successful hardback, *Tycoons: Where They Came From and How They Made It*, one of our own ideas, by William Kay, the business editor of *The Times*. The book profiled a number of hugely successful self-made British tycoons (regretfully all men as we were unable at that time to discover any women), nearly all of whom had been self-starters.

The late 1980s had been a stable time for people employed in the workplace, but all that was to change. The recession of the early 1990s was different from that of the early 1980s in that this time it affected white-collar workers, many of whom had had no previous experience of finding themselves out of work. Faced with the need to cut costs, many employers kept their female staff on because they were cheaper to employ; it was the male white-collar workers who suffered the most. Everyone knew someone who had been made redundant. Some people never got back on their feet. While many companies were hurting, the recession presented a multitude of opportunities for Piatkus, which we did our best to grasp. We kept a very careful watch on our overheads but gradually began to move our publishing programme in a new and exciting direction.

During the 1980s, Piatkus was particularly known for titles of interest to women in the areas of cookery, beauty and health, but since we had launched the company, women had entered the workforce in much greater numbers. For many it was now not a choice but a financial necessity. The price of housing and everyday expenses was rising, salaries were not keeping up and it was becoming common for both parents to have to go out to work. These women, making their own money and making buying decisions in a way they hadn't before, were a new and previously untapped consumer market and it had become possible to target books to them in new and creative ways. We had a head start on many other publishing companies because we had so many women on our staff and had been marketing to our women customers for many years already.

The marketing of all books was also changing, along with the growth of marketing itself. As selling became more sophisticated, by the end of the 1980s I wondered if I should take a marketing course. It took a while for me to realize that we were already marketing our books quite naturally and it wasn't until early in the 1990s that we employed our first in-house marketing manager. Before the existence of the internet, there were many fewer channels through which to market our books. There was only a handful of television channels and although commercial radio was growing, it was very fragmented. There was the national press and a huge range of specialist magazines. Although there were always women feature writers, it took a while for many of the national newspapers to appreciate how they might better address their women readers directly. The *Daily Mail* was one of the first to do this when it launched its Femail pages.

An audit of our strengths and weaknesses had shown us clearly that major problems were lying ahead for us in our specialist areas. Rival publishers with deep pockets and teams of experienced staff were producing very attractive, full-colour, lavishly illustrated and designed cookbooks and health books. We knew we couldn't compete and looked around for inspiration. What could we publish that would work for us editorially and financially with our small staff and limited capital? The answer, as so often in the company's history, came from the changes in the society around us and how our own families and friends were being affected – and this is where the recession became an opportunity for us. Everyone was anxious about their job security so people were wanting to improve their skills in the workplace either to retain their jobs or to help them find new ones. We realized there was a market for self-help and business books targeted at the layperson – as opposed to the academic textbook market.

Our first success in this new business book market was *The Perfect CV* by Tom Jackson. It was an American large-format book, A4 in size, which explained not only how to compile and write a CV but also included numerous examples of how to set it out so that your skills were displayed to best advantage. Nowadays there are lots of companies who will help you write your CV, but in the early 1990s those organizations didn't exist. *The Perfect CV* sold well because it was the best book on the market and was bought by many people who had never had to write a CV before.

Our growing export market became very important for all the new business and self-help titles. Over the years since Philip had joined the company, the range of new and backlist titles that he had to sell had grown considerably. After moving into the new office building, we had been able to take on more people to assist him and, as a result, we were building a powerful sales team. In 1990 we were joined by Diane Hill, who started with us as our sales manager with responsibility for our UK turnover. Diane, a superb and energetic saleswoman, always had a smile on her face and fitted into our fast-expanding team very quickly. She had come from a large corporation and liked the idea of working for a smaller company. Philip had worked to build an effective enthusiastic sales force overseas. When our list had been new and small, we had worked with smaller companies in our different export markets, but as it grew, our publishing programme became much more attractive to larger companies with more powerful sales teams, who were particularly interested to work with us because we published so many popular American books, which usually sold well in every foreign market. Philip built up good relationships with book distributors in those territories where, in common with other British publishing houses, we usually had an exclusive licence to sell our titles: Australia, New Zealand, South Africa, Canada and the Far East. Cookery and parenting books had never done well in these territories but when we began to publish our business, self-help, popular psychology and mind, body, spirit books, the global markets were keen to buy them.

Our export sales took us into new territory financially. It was a mixed blessing. When we achieved a large export order for a book, our initial print run would run into several thousand copies. In the UK, we were paid by our customers after two or three months, but when we shipped copies abroad we could wait to be paid for four to six months, which could put a lot of pressure on the cash flow. However, our export sales had a major upside: their contribution to a print run brought the print cost of each book down.

I would remind myself of old business maxims I had learned at the beginning of my publishing career. One was "you have to pay to play"; another was "if you can't stand the heat, get out of the kitchen". I had chosen to grow my company without any outside help and the cash-flow challenge was the price I was paying. By now, though, I was confident that if anything happened to me, the company would have value to a buyer because we had a number of successful titles that were continuing to sell. It was this knowledge that stopped me from lying awake at night. I loved what I did, and, working together, our small management team controlled what we did. No one could tell us what to do. All we had to do was stay on top of the game.

Dealing with Difficult People was our second business experiment that sold well. Today there are several books with similar titles but early in the 1990s that concept was a first. *The Complete Time Management System*, *Confident Conversation*, *The Complete Book of Business Etiquette*, *How to Win Customers and Keep Them for Life*, *Making Profits*, *Managing Your Team* and many more followed; all solid workplace skills with a clear, targeted market. Many of the ideas in the books changed our own behaviour, sharpening our focus and offering us nuggets of wisdom. The books sold well through both retail and specialist outlets, including the Business Book Club which was also having a boom in this challenging market. On several occasions, the book clubs chose our titles as their specialist main selections, giving us larger than usual orders for what were, for us, expensive hardbacks.

We also published books about making money and getting rich. I liked reading those myself because I was always looking for new ways to try to increase our profits. *Think and Grow Rich* was a classic by Napoleon Hill and, although we didn't publish that title, we did publish several other books of his. In later years, *Secrets of the Millionaire Mind* by T. Harv Eker, *Getting Everything You Can Out of All You've Got* by Jay Abraham and several books by marketing guru Seth Godin were among my favourite motivational business books on the Piatkus list. I would often sit at home on one of my reading days with a notebook by my side, reflecting on how I could transfer their wisdom to our enterprise. As I came across interesting ideas, I would go to the computer and mail my colleagues with questions, ideas and suggestions (they weren't expected to reply immediately). Reading all these business books was very valuable in expanding our own thinking.

The mid-1990s was also a time when people began to think more seriously about getting on the property ladder. Housing was much more affordable in relation to salaries than it is now. People were being helped and encouraged to buy their own homes, and the price of property began to soar. We published *The Streetwise Guide to Buying and Selling Your Home* for this market. We had a particularly good freelance sales representative, David, who sold into the airport bookshops for us. I remember going on holiday and being thrilled to see how many of our books were for sale in WHSmith and the other bookshop outlets in the airport terminal at that time. At one point – before our rivals had caught up and began to compete so heavily in the genres of business books and self-help titles – we were really ahead of the game. It was very exciting.

It has always been hard to make a good living in the publishing industry. We could price our business books higher than the books targeted solely at women, but they were still paperbacks. By the time the bookshop, the wholesalers, the author and the distributor had taken their cut of the sales of a business paperback priced at £12.99 or £14.99, there wasn't much money left for us. It has always been like that in general book publishing, but it did mean that it was very hard to build a company and to do better each year than the previous one. We were never able to rest on our laurels, something we often repeated to ourselves to avoid becoming over-arrogant when we did have a good year.

We also continued to struggle to persuade some British literary agents and some of the American companies to offer us books. It was frustrating as we had become experts in certain areas of publishing and there were books that we knew we could publish better than some of our larger competitors. But there were always some snobby literary agents who didn't want to deal with us because we weren't Penguin, Random House or HarperCollins. They wanted the highest possible advances for their authors, without realizing the value of a small company's expertise and dedication. Our advances were usually only a little lower, but Jana and our sales team continued to work on promoting our books long after their publication dates and this became one of our USPs. All our authors were generally very happy that the continuing publicity might sometimes generate ongoing income for them and help them to become increasingly better known in their field of expertise. Over the years, long after we'd been the underbidder for a book, many authors would tell me that they wished they had been published by us. But by then it was too late. We concentrated our efforts on authors who had faith in us and that faith was often rewarded in every way that counted.

Aside from business, the other area where we had begun to make our mark at the beginning of the 1990s recession was in the popular psychology market, which was still in its infancy in the UK. The books we published in this area also began to have a profound impact on me. I read voraciously, picking out for our list not necessarily the ones I liked but the ones I thought we could sell. (It was difficult to gauge which American books would be of interest to British readers. Some of them were way ahead in their thinking and ideas.)

There is a saying "when the student is ready, the teacher appears". I didn't know I was so hungry for knowledge about my internal life. Suddenly this huge influx of books about the psyche was food and drink to me. I was gobbling them up voraciously, whether I thought we could publish them or not. I was reading everything we were offered and many books that other British companies were publishing. (It was always important to know what our rivals were up to.) I was learning so much about the internal workings of my own life. My mind was being opened to so much knowledge. I often made mistakes, though, not always trusting myself to know which problems were universal.

Reading *The Dance of Anger* by Harriet G. Lerner enabled me to confront my mother for the first time. I was thirty-seven and I was able to ask her not to criticize me. After my request, which took a lot of courage, she did stop for a while. But then her criticisms came at me less overtly and more like sharp daggers when I was least expecting them. It felt to me as if she was still disappointed in me for not being the perfect daughter of her fantasies. But after reading the book, I was no longer so cowed by her. I had learned that there were different and more subtle techniques for trying to manage our relationship.

The Dance of Anger was such a good book, but the American publisher who was offering it to us didn't want us to sell copies in our usual export markets. Reluctantly, I felt unable to buy the rights for it and, every now and again, I would feel very sad that we couldn't always buy all of the books we wanted, even when we were offered them. One day, I sat in the office and looked at the title of a book we had been offered and thought, "That sounds too American. We will never be able to sell it here." I didn't even bother to read it. It was a big mistake and one I regretted for years to come. *Feel the Fear and Do It Anyway* by Susan Jeffers went on to sell hundreds and thousands of copies – but not for us. Luckily, and for a reason I can't remember now, we were offered the opportunity to publish other titles by the author, and this time we didn't turn them down. It was a lesson to me that we had to look at everything that arrived on our desks, no matter how strange the title.

Another book that had a profound effect on me was by Louis Proto, who sadly died of AIDS a short while after we published his third book. His specialist topics included the mind–body connection and self-esteem. His was the first book that introduced me to the concept of self-love. Nowadays there are so many writers exploring how to love yourself, but at that time Louis's work felt profoundly new and mind-expanding to me. In order for the reader to learn to love themselves, instructed Louis in one exercise, they must stand in front of a mirror, look themselves in the face directly and say "I love you" three times out loud – and of course mean it as they said it. It took me a long time to be able to do it. At first, I could only get one sentence out and then I shuddered and felt embarrassed. It was quite ridiculous. How could anyone love themselves? How could I love myself? Yuk. Yet over the years I would remember the exercise and, every now and again, I would give it another go. One day, I realized that I could do it. I could look at myself and feel love for myself. I had left behind the little girl who had so often been criticized by my mother for not being perfect, for never being good enough. I could now accept myself as I was, indeed as I am, both with my good qualities and all my faults.

SEVENTEEN
NEW AGE

At the beginning of the 1990s, books in the mind, body, spirit category were shelved in bookshops under the heading "New Age", a term that originated in America. In the UK, they were perceived as being very American in tone and content, somewhat suspect in their ideas and therefore very "woo-woo". There was a whiff of snobbery in those who disdained them, especially in the UK, and many larger publishers didn't want to be seen to be publishing them. As a nation, we were not used to sharing our emotions. The concept of the stiff upper lip still prevailed and these New Age ideas felt very un-British.

With our track record for frequently publishing the kind of books many other publishers didn't want – romantic novels and books about alternative therapies and popular psychology – we were eager to be offered as many books in this new genre as were available. We had previously gained some experience in this genre by publishing a few books on astrology and psychic development, including three by Jonathan Cainer, who was to become the hugely successful astrologer at the *Daily Mail*, but by that point astrology was almost mainstream. Now there were so many new opportunities coming our way. Such was our enthusiasm that we soon became one of the first English publishing houses people began to think of for these books. Until that time, Thorsons (which was now owned by William Collins) and Rider (which was owned by Random House) had been among the few go-to-publishers in this area. Hodder were also building a small but exceptionally good list, with authors such as Eckhart Tolle and Neale Donald Walsch. But these companies couldn't publish everything, so Piatkus Books didn't have a problem gradually building a publishing programme in the mind, body, spirit area. We knew there was a market for the books; the major challenge was how to reach it.

It took a while for the shops to recognize the size of this largely untapped market. The impact of the recession became the factor that opened it up. After people had lost their jobs or had fought hard to keep them, and after they had acquired new skills, they had often been through a gruelling few years. Now it was time to heal from the experience of being out of work and short of money, and ask the question, "Why did this happen to me?"

One of our home-grown authors in the mind, body, spirit field, Soozi Holbeche, was an expert on healing with crystals and semi-precious stones. A beautiful and elegant Englishwoman, who always looked as if she would be at home at a Buckingham Palace garden party, Soozi had built up a following and gave regular workshops. Susan, an enthusiastic editor who had recently joined the company and who was interested in this area, encouraged us to commission Soozi's first book, *The Power of Gems and Crystals*, and I read it at proof stage and found it very interesting. What I didn't realize was that it had been given to me to read without the introductory chapter, which Soozi hadn't yet delivered.

The book was due to be published in the autumn of 1990 and I read it a few months before then while lying on the sofa in my office. Cyril and I had been learning to play golf and in our final lesson I'd swung round too enthusiastically with the golf club. It was to be a movement that changed my life. I felt an ache for a couple of days and then we went to the cinema one evening and I sat still for two hours. The next morning I woke up and could not move. I could hardly walk the few steps to the bathroom, I was in such pain. I had never experienced anything like it before. I was a healthy young woman and thought the pain would go after a few days' bed rest. It didn't. A friend's mother recommended her osteopath, who diagnosed it as a pinched sciatic nerve. He assured me it would get better but it would take time and more treatment sessions.

I returned home from the appointment and dragged myself upstairs. The pain was acute and remained so for several days; often the only relief was to lie on the floor clutching a bag of frozen peas to the base of my spine. As I gradually began to be able to move a little more, I slithered downstairs to sit in a chair. The effort exhausted me; I felt completely debilitated. After a couple of weeks I had to return to work because there was so much to do. In the days before computers it was hard to work from home. Three days a week, Cyril would drive me to the office early in the morning before he went to work and I would struggle up the three flights of stairs and collapse onto a small sofa, where I would lie for hours, even in meetings. At the end of the day, holding tightly to the bannisters, I would pull myself downstairs to the ground floor and into a waiting minicab.

It was and has been the most painful injury of my life so far, and the healing process went on for several months. The experience was important because it taught me that the body heals in its own time; it has its own way of working and its timetable is unknown. You can't fight the pain; you can't hurry your healing. You have to learn to let go and surrender and, once you do that, you need only to relax and wait. You will get better if you allow yourself the time.

It was suggested to me that Soozi might be able to help my back to heal, so I made an appointment with her. By then, I was able to travel in a cab to her small flat in Kew. There were beautiful crystals on every surface. It felt very soothing. She invited me to lie down on the spotless white bedspread in her bedroom and began to tell me what she would do.

Because I hadn't read the first chapter of her book, I hadn't realized that Soozi, as well as working with crystals, was also an expert in past-life regression therapy. I was about to be regressed to look at my past lives in order to find out why I had such severe back pain. It was a shock to discover what was about to happen, but because I was her publisher – supposed to know what she did and had written about – I couldn't admit to it. Obediently, I closed my eyes and Soozi began a guided meditation which took me back into a previous life.

After an hour, the experience ended. Soozi had regressed me to three separate lives and she had given me a healing meditation to help me get well. She was not only trying to heal my physical pain but also some of my childhood wounds. During the experience, I saw myself as a male leader of men centuries ago, perhaps somewhere in Scandinavia – I was dressed as I imagined a Viking would be – and I had not behaved as a leader should. I had also had very different, contrasting lives in Egypt, where I had been a pampered princess in one and an outcast in another. We discussed whether and how these experiences might be impacting on my present life.

Soozi included meditation and visualization in her session to enable me to begin to make a full recovery from not only the physical pain with my back but also the emotional issues with my parents, which had affected so much of how I had experienced my life up until that time. She explained to me about our souls and our spirits, our past lives and our karma. All this was a lot to take in, yet it felt very powerful and interesting. It was as if a door had opened for me to a completely new way of seeing and experiencing the world. It was going to take some time to absorb and I hoped it would help to make me well. I went home and wrote up everything I could remember so that I could reflect on the experience in the weeks and months ahead.

There was a special postscript to the year 1990. My pinched sciatic nerve had happened in the spring; by autumn, although I was much better, Cyril was still driving me to work so that I wouldn't use up all my energy on the tube journey. One morning in October, he drove me to the Ritz in Piccadilly for a networking breakfast hosted by the International Women's Forum, an organization for senior women executives. It had started off like an ordinary morning, but by the time he dropped me off at the Ritz we had decided to get married. I had left home a single woman; now, forty minutes later, I was engaged to be married. It wasn't exactly the kind of romantic proposal I had spent much of my career reading about. But it felt right. We were both very happy.

We had a small wedding at the end of that year, surrounded by friends and family. I still couldn't stand up straight for long and had to sit on a chair for part of the ceremony. In spite of the pragmatic proposal, my husband has turned out to be the most romantic of men. He must have read some of our books when I wasn't looking.

EIGHTEEN

MANAGING PEOPLE

As an SME – small to medium-sized company – Piatkus probably made every kind of mistake possible in the twenty-five years or more of our independent existence. After some years, inspired no doubt by all the personal growth books we were reading and publishing, we learned to treat every mistake as a learning opportunity. What was interesting, though, was how far ahead of our time we were in our flexible workplace policies. Because I was a working mother, a single parent of three children, I appreciated all the problems of trying to combine work and career with a happy, well-functioning home life. When we interviewed job applicants we would say to them, "We want you to come in every morning and work hard from nine to five, then go home and have a life." We believed that, in a creative organization, it was essential that people had time to relax and refresh, and were able to think about what was going on in the world other than work. Only in that way would they have the energy to bring good ideas back to the company, no matter in which department they worked.

Sometimes in our Monday editorial meetings, I would ask everyone what they and their friends had been discussing over the weekend; it kept us informed about the zeitgeist and gave us lots of ideas for future book projects. Of course, as with all companies, sometimes we hired the wrong people. We would review CVs and invite all the shortlisted applicants to at least one interview and sometimes two – and would give them a short test to assess their skills. One time, we advertised for a fiction editorial assistant and all the candidates had to proofread a jacket blurb that we had especially designed to make it difficult to check. More than 150 applications were sent in and we created a shortlist of eight people, whom we interviewed (all of them with relevant experience in either publishing or bookshops). Only one candidate, who had been working in a bookshop, completed the task accurately and we hired her immediately. We tried not to take on people who were applying for their first job as we were so stretched we couldn't afford the time to teach them the basic skills; interns weren't taken on either, as having them work without earning a salary did not feel right to us.

During the interviews, we would explain that working in a small company was very different from working in a larger organization. All employees were expected to muck in, including taking a lunch-hour turn on reception or being part of the rota to answer the phone if the receptionist was on a call. We employed a student or part-timer to organize our post and take it to the post office, but staff were invariably expected to pack their own parcels if they were in a hurry to get something off. There was no hierarchy about making coffee; I was usually to be seen with a mug in hand and had no problem making a drink for anyone else. Employees from larger companies sometimes struggled to adjust to this informal style of management.

At Piatkus, our employment policy was to work with freelancers as much as possible and this policy contributed to keeping us very lean. When we did decide we were ready to take on another full-time employee, we always did our best to hire the best person for the job and, as long as we thought they would be relaxed and flexible enough to fit in with our company culture, we followed our usual strategy. We used to joke that none of the three principal directors had been to university, but we did of course require all staff to be educated to a certain standard as we were a publishing company, working with the written word. We didn't discriminate and the people we hired appreciated this and were frequently open about their gender identity, background and culture. We enjoyed nurturing people's talents and giving them opportunities to expand their capabilities. It was lovely to see people blossom. Gill, Philip, Simon and Diane were all particularly good at managing people and building loyal teams. We didn't have a high staff turnover and there was always a lot of affection for their time at Piatkus from people who had worked in the company, gained knowledge and experience, and had then gone on to achieve satisfying and fulfilling careers in other organizations. We loved seeing our former colleagues succeed in their careers as they grew older and matured. Every now and then we would hold a reunion party for present and former staff and our most loyal long-term freelancers. It was always good to see how people were getting on and to stay in touch with them.

We usually had more women working for us than men and I do remember when we once had three women in the company who were pregnant at the same time and one expectant father (to whom we offered paternity leave, which hadn't at that time been written into UK law). It was a year when we found ourselves with a lot of books about expectant mothers and parenting on offer. Luckily the babies weren't all due at the same time.

In the 1980s and 1990s, publishing was – and, indeed, still is – run mainly by middle- and upper-class white men in their fifties and sixties. Although many women worked in the industry, there were very few at the top. I wasn't the first woman to launch her own company: Marion Boyars of Calder and Boyars, Margaret Busby of Allison & Busby, Kyle Cathie with her eponymous company, and Victoria Barnsley at Fourth Estate also held the flag for women publishers in the 1980s but, in reality, there were not many of us. Several of the most successful literary agents were women and they did a lot to correct the balance, especially when they represented very successful authors.

Another area where our policies were ahead of our time was in our flexible attitude to the hours people could work. Not long after we left the Loughton house and moved to town, Jane, who had been with the company for several years by then, asked if she could work from seven in the morning until early afternoon. Her husband would take their little boy to school and she would leave early to pick him up. We agreed to try it. A few years later, Simon followed her example, working from eight until four, so he could avoid the rush hour when he and his family moved out to a village near Cambridge. We were concerned at first that this early end to his working day would impact on how he worked with the printing companies, but we soon realized many of the factories worked similar hours and it turned out not to be a problem at all. Jana worked in the office Tuesdays and Thursdays, but was always flexible when necessary, and Gill and I regularly took a reading day at home each week. As our editorial department expanded, more senior staff were also given permission to work from home every now and then. We trusted people not to abuse the privilege – and they didn't.

Being flexible where we could and listening to our staff made for a much happier team. At one point, we had two young women in the company who wanted to swap their roles after realizing they wanted to experience working in different departments. If a person was feeling aggrieved, we always tried to act quickly to put things right; as the number of people on the staff expanded, we realized that in such a small and close-knit community it was easy for one person to impact on the energy of the company in a negative way. If someone was critical and undermining of what we, as an organization, were trying to do, we tried to find out what their grievances were and sort them out. We learned that it is often the small things that can be easily remedied which make a huge difference, so we tried to have as few rules and regulations as possible and to treat people as individuals – very much as we would like to be treated if we were them. If hardworking employees needed the odd day off to go to a funeral or were late because they were waiting for the plumber, we didn't feel the need to keep a record. We trusted people and it was only very rarely that anyone took advantage of that trust. We believed that if you look after the small things, people would feel they had some ownership in what we were all together working to achieve. There was a kettle in the corner of each of the office floors and we would order people's preferred teas and coffees, within reason. The stationery was kept under lock and key but we were never mean with it. Everyone was allowed to take home a copy of any book we published if they wanted to read it or give it to a member of their family.

At one of our regular meetings, Dennis, our external marketing consultant, made the observation that our culture was very different from that of a corporate organization. I asked him to be more specific. "It's the way everyone talks to one another," he said. "You talk as if you were a family." At the time I didn't appreciate exactly what he meant but several years later, when I found myself taking part in a few corporate meetings, I understood. At Piatkus, we had a relaxed culture and people were always being encouraged to say what they thought. Even if they were sometimes a little reluctant to speak up, we did want to hear everyone's opinions. If Philip and I disagreed about a strategy for a book we would often express ourselves quite openly in a marketing or sales meeting. We both knew we were on the same side – wanting to find the best way to make each book a success – and in order to do that we needed to speak freely. I realized that it could be quite surprising at first for people who had come from the corporate world and weren't used to our frank and direct comments.

As new changes to employment law evolved, we had, of necessity, to become more bureaucratic and develop our own rules and policies. Simon was in charge of keeping these records for the company and put together a "black book". In the 1980s, it was just a few pages. By the time we sold the company in 2007, it had, inevitably, become a substantial volume. While as an entrepreneur I was always a risk-taker, as a manager I was always cautious. My more risk-averse side was always concerned that it would cost a lot of time and money that we could ill afford if we broke any employment laws. As employment legislation became more complex and onerous, we hired a specialist HR company on a monthly retainer so that they could be on hand if we needed expert guidance. Fortunately, in our twenty-five year existence we only had one massive run-in with an employment tribunal. Although the case was settled in our favour shortly before it went to the tribunal, it was nevertheless hugely time- and energy-consuming.

The very worst part of being an owner-manager and running a company was when we had to let people go. It wasn't so bad if they weren't doing their job well, because we knew that it was in the interests of the company as a whole. When an employee is under-performing, everyone inside the company (and often outside) knows it. The staff want you as managers to do something about it and, however much they might like their colleague, there is always a huge sense of relief when they hear that the person has been asked to leave.

Conversely, it is the worst possible experience to have to ask bright, committed and talented people to go. Fortunately, there were only a couple of times in our history when we had no other option but to do so. At one point, when the market had begun to contract for a certain type of book, a complete restructure of our non-fiction editorial department was required. We went through the regulatory consultancy period, which is always very stressful for everyone. However, it wasn't all bad, as during the consultation period two of the employees suggested how they might continue to work with us in different roles and so we were able to continue our working relationship with them, albeit in a new way. I do remember this period as being one of the low points of my working life, but we'd had to act in the interests of the company as a whole and had no other choice.

NINETEEN

MORE MISTAKES

Piatkus Books had been in existence about twelve years when we decided to employ our first management consultant in the early 1990s. We had grown from a one-woman band, pregnant and working from a desk in her bedroom, to a competent and respected organization that had achieved a turnover of several million pounds, with no outside financial support aside from our constantly increasing bank overdraft. In fact, it hadn't occurred to us to look for any, in the same way we hadn't thought we might need a board with non-executive directors. When it came to sign the audited accounts, only my signature was required. We thought we were doing perfectly well, making up our own management rules as we went along.

We only began to realize how much we still had to learn about running a great business after our business book range began to flourish and we were offered interesting titles to publish. We decided to ask one of our management authors, Malcolm Bird, to review the company for us. He interviewed all of us and Gill, Philip and I assembled to hear his verdict. He told us that we were doing pretty well, all things considered, but we weren't holding enough meetings. As a result, a lot of time was being wasted because we weren't passing on information as efficiently as we could be. Having always tried not to have too many meetings – the bane of so many larger organizations – we had to laugh. Malcolm suggested we instigate regular weekly meetings, in all the key departments, which didn't have to be very long; and if we held brief standing meetings without chairs it would further shorten the process. Each head of department put in place the kind of meeting they thought they needed. Being a hands-on publisher, I needed to be involved in several of them myself. Always aware how much it was costing to have so many people in the room, I tried to encourage everyone to get through their agendas as quickly as they could. Anyway, they soon learned that if the meetings dragged on too long I would get bored and then it was hard to contain my irritability.

Fiction editorial meetings were very straightforward. Throughout the history of the company there were only ever two people making decisions: a senior fiction executive editor and myself. If one of us found a new and interesting author, we would discuss them together. Sometimes we would send the novel to an outside reader for a third opinion. After that, we would make a decision. If it was a novel by an author we had previously published, our conversation would be about how much profit (or loss) the previous book had made and whether we thought we would be able to increase their market profile and sales. We were always keen to sign a first novel if we could. While they were always more risky to publish, at least there was no sales track record to hinder buyers getting behind it, and booksellers tended to be enthusiastic about finding an exciting new voice.

Non-fiction editorial decisions were much more complex. Unlike fiction, each book could be published in a variety of formats and price points. Our costings were therefore much more complicated. There might be drawings or colour illustrations to price in, as well as various qualities of paper, a more complex page design and index. In addition, some of these books required a significant marketing budget. The non-fiction team would start the week with a brief progress update for all the books in the forthcoming schedule, followed by a senior editors' meeting, before, finally, one with the sales department. Diane's opinion was critical to our decision-making; if we, the editors, couldn't persuade our sales team that they could sell a book, then we knew they wouldn't be able to persuade their customers to buy it. If she and Philip didn't like something we put forward, or if we found that the numbers weren't adding up and the book didn't look as if it could make a profit, we would discuss it again at the next editorial meeting to see if there was a different way of presenting it. We might consider a more standard format, fewer illustrations or a higher price point. There are always so many ways to publish a single idea.

When cash flow was tight and we were short of money, we had a system whereby we would designate the categories A, B or C to a book. An "A" book would make a profit for us based on previous information – such as being by one of our bestselling authors on a hot topic – and we had no hesitation in making an offer. A "B" book was questionable, and a "C" would be too marginal. When we had more money in the bank, we could take a chance on more "B" books, which were necessary to our company because all creative industries must continue to innovate. The simple ABC system worked well for the whole buying team as everyone could understand it.

My most hated meeting was our weekly cover meeting. The book cover is the most important part of the sales process, but I am not a visual person and struggled to view covers objectively. I found that I needed to place them face out on a bookshelf to get any real sense of whether they would work. (Of course, many books are sold spine out so that had to be taken into consideration too.)

Covers are hugely subjective. We might select a preference at the cover meeting but our author's taste might not coincide with ours. Bestselling authors who have cover consultation and approval written into their contracts were an especial challenge if we didn't all agree. Sometimes we had to go back to the drawing board and start again from scratch, which was both expensive and time-consuming, as well as demoralizing for the editor in charge of that book.

After we had established what our estimated sales figures might be at home and overseas, including book clubs and libraries, as well as possible foreign rights income, we costed the project. We had devised a basic costing system and Simon, together with our financial manager, would work out the potential profit and loss. This could take a few days for a book that wasn't a standard format. After that, we would have a further discussion about the book, making sure we were all in agreement about the best way to publish it, before making an offer. Earlier in my publishing career I had frequently made mistakes by squandering too much money on advances for some titles. For us, that might be as much as £10,000 for a book for which we really should only have paid £3,000 or £5,000. When I visited America I would sometimes get swayed – and excited – by a savvy sales pitch from an American publisher. At the Frankfurt Book Fair, it was difficult to avoid getting caught up in a bidding frenzy, although star editors from larger companies, eager to make their mark (and spending Other People's Money), made many more expensive mistakes than we ever did. Over the years, the practice of holding auctions at the Frankfurt fair gradually died down and many books got sold just before it, or bound proof copies would be taken back home to be read in the weeks following. Older and wiser heads had prevailed, the industry was becoming more sophisticated and every company was taking much longer to make decisions.

I wasn't betting the roof of the house. Most books that were offered to us were also offered to several other companies at the same time. We would sometimes get a call from a literary agent telling us they had an offer for a book we had also been sent. We would try to wheedle the figure out of them, and then it was an added skill – which we weren't always very good at – trying to work out which other company had offered and how much they might have put on the table. We then had to factor in the time and money we were liable to waste rushing around doing costings, only to find that we weren't the highest bidder anyway. I did sometimes break the rules if I came across a book that I was very enthusiastic about. This was not always a good idea, frequently leading me to pay advances that were higher than they should have been. But usually not high enough to cause a car crash.

In the early 1990s, when we were still publishing new cookery titles from Mary Berry and Pat Chapman, owner of the Curry Club, and new books by Mary Spillane of the UK Colour Me Beautiful organization, we knew that larger companies were circling, tempted to poach our top authors with higher advances and larger marketing budgets. We appreciated how loyal these authors were to us and would offer as large an advance as we could afford, albeit knowing that we could wake up one morning and learn that one of our most profitable stars, whose work and reputation we had spent years building, had decided to leave. Always mindful of that possibility, we needed to be constantly on our toes, looking to discover talented new authors and brands at the beginning of their life and to publish these books in such a way that the authors would want to remain with us.

Some managing directors are numbers-oriented and hire creative people to work alongside them. Others are more creative, not always so hot about the figures. At Piatkus, the editors and I were the intuitive creatives. This meant that we hadn't always paid as much attention to the numbers as we should. We didn't ignore them but sometimes our enthusiasm overrode common sense when we fell in love with a particular book, one that wasn't really quite right for our programme. Having more meetings enabled us to become more focused as a team, working together more effectively to achieve the best outcome. It is a truism in publishing that most books that are published by general publishers don't make a profit. Publishing is not an exact science so inevitably many wrong decisions are made. For the first fifteen years, we operated on instinct and intuition. If we thought we could make a success of a book, we would have a go – a strategy that had been very successful in our early years. But that had been when author advances were affordable.

In the second half of the 1980s, we had experimented with a wide range of titles and had become good at publishing books in certain areas. But although many were selling enough copies to enable us to keep reprinting them, they weren't necessarily making us much money. There isn't a standard way of doing this in publishing, but, eventually, we learned to refine our financial system and cost our books more accurately. We might not always have been as tightly focused as we should have been with our publishing decisions, but we were very self-disciplined in our accounting procedures, writing down the value of all our advances in the month of publication. This meant we never deluded ourselves into thinking we were doing better as a company than we actually were. In practice, we always knew when we were doing well as cash was not so tight. It didn't matter what the value of our books in the warehouse was on paper; if people didn't want to buy them, they might as well have had no value at all.

A couple of times a year we would publish a book because we felt passionately about it, as long as we thought it would break even. We took the view that, as we were an independent publishing house and we cared about good writing and new ideas, it was important that we sometimes published a book because we wanted to put it out there. One time we were offered a beautiful but also controversial memoir by an American author who was not then known in Britain. It was the story of how she had become pregnant with a Down's syndrome child and how so many people who knew her had encouraged her to have an abortion. I was entranced by the way the author wrote. I loved her style, her use of language, and was moved to tears when I read her story. We discussed the book in detail at the editorial meeting. It wouldn't be an expensive purchase. We probably talked about an advance of £3,000. Eventually, it was decided that as I loved it so much, we should take a chance and publish it.

The book was *Expecting Adam* and the author was Martha Beck, who later became internationally known as lifestyle coach to the American television star Oprah Winfrey. We sent out advance proofs to magazine editors and to colleagues who were selling books into the export market. Our South African export agency had a female sales director who also fell in love with the book. Her passion and enthusiasm for it meant that our South African colleagues at Penguin Books, who were selling our programme in that market, marked it out for special attention. *Expecting Adam* became a word-of-mouth book, a huge bestseller there, and it made a lovely profit for us. I was always happy when risky books made a profit. But what I loved more than anything was thinking about the pleasure the writers were able to give to such a large audience.

TWENTY
BECOMING A
PAPERBACK PUBLISHER

In the first ten years of Piatkus's existence, huge changes had taken place in the world of books, as well as in the commercial world outside the book trade. Authors were paid far greater sums of money than before and although smaller publishers such as ourselves found ourselves priced out of the market very often, sometimes this worked in our favour. Some authors had a popular following in the library market but their bookshop sales were diminishing; we were always happy to take them on so they could continue writing. In due course, they received an additional income from the new Public Lending Right bill, which stipulated that every author whose book was borrowed from a library should receive a small payment.

Standing on the sidelines, witnessing all the consolidation, was fascinating. During the 1980s, it seemed as if there were a company sale every month. Sometimes the fallout was massive: so many redundancies and new hirings. The publishing trade had always been gossipy; now, people were having a field day. However, the industry is a fairly small one. At the same time as people were observing the changes, with dismay or schadenfreude, they also knew that their junior team member today might end up being their boss tomorrow. It was a very uncertain time.

Until the mid-1980s, most paperback books had been published in the same small format. Now a new, more literary genre of fiction had arrived and was being published in a slightly larger "B" format. Piatkus Books had been selling some of our fiction to the paperback houses, but we could see that this way of publishing would soon come to an end. More and more companies were preferring to publish vertically, buying the rights to publish in all formats and then not selling any of those rights to their UK publishing competitors. We decided to try to develop our own paperback list. We had some excellent novels in our backlist with which we wanted to experiment, even though several of the authors were not well known. Devoting much time and energy to the books and their marketing, we devised a cover format with what we thought were eye-catching yellow and pink stripes. The series was well received by reviewers, and bookshops agreed to try them. By the publication date for the first books, we were heartened by our pre-publication sales. In the publishing industry virtually all books are sold on a sale-or-return basis. Sadly the series did not sell very well and many booksellers returned to us the stock that they had ordered.

We had made many mistakes with this new venture. The novels didn't look right in the format we had chosen for them; the covers were garish and ugly. We had made the classic mistake of not showing the new designs to our major customers (that is, WHSmith, Waterstones and the other key bookshop chains at that time) beforehand to solicit their opinions. The only reason they took the books for their stores was because they liked us and wanted to give us their support. Had we asked their opinions earlier, they would surely have sent us back to the drawing board very quickly. It was a painful but much needed lesson for us. We had chosen good books but had packaged and marketed them wrongly. The next time we tried to publish in paperback we would make sure that we worked collaboratively with our customers and got the basics right.

TWENTY ONE

THE YEARS OF PLENTY

The mid-1990s were a very happy time. As a wife, mother and businesswoman, I really did feel like I had it all. Sonia was settled in her home at the Village and was making good progress. She went to school on site and was having fun enjoying art, cookery and swimming lessons. She was even learning computing and, with help, was able to press down on a large, specially designed button on the keyboard, which enabled her to create a simple jingle with pictures on the screen. She had always loved music and would listen attentively to every new record we played her when she was young. Now she was having playlists of her favourite music made for her. She was also having regular physiotherapy; we could see her muscles getting stronger. She was in a good place.

The two younger children, now aged fourteen and twelve, were settled at their secondary schools. Money was sometimes a bit short. I owned the company but was always cautious about how much I could actually afford to pay myself. I took a monthly salary along with everyone else but not a huge one. In good years I was able to take a bonus but sometimes there wasn't enough cash in the bank to pay it. I would have to pay tax on the bonus and leave the money in the company until we could afford for me to take it out.

Now it was Cyril's turn to work from home. We had used all our savings to move to a larger house in Stanmore on the outskirts of North London, with bigger bedrooms and a sizeable loft extension. It had a charming garden that supposedly backed onto a deer park, but beautiful tall trees hid our view so we could never see any deer. Now our roles were reversed: Cyril was building a business, manufacturing and importing disposable gloves from the Far East and, this time, it was he who would be using the attic as his office. The children felt they were too old for a nanny so Cyril would take them to school in the morning, doing a rota with another mother in our street, and they would come home on the school bus.

As Cyril's business grew, he began to take on part-time staff. After the children and I left in the morning, several ladies who lived locally would come into the house to work alongside him, using telesales techniques to sell his gloves out of the loft extension. They were very pleasant women, all working different hours and on different days. As I was usually away at the office myself, I would occasionally meet them on the stairs, when one of them was either arriving or leaving. It always amused me that both Cyril and I had started our own ventures in the same way, by having a relaxed working arrangement with other people in our home.

Matthew and Leah had become very independent. They had long been used to making their own arrangements, telling their father when they would be visiting him on the weekends (if they didn't have a party invitation or something on at school) and planning time out with friends. If something needed to be organized, they had to do it themselves as there was no one to do it for them. This was before everyone had a mobile phone and could ring or text or FaceTime. They had both become very practical, learning to cook and clean, make their beds and hoover. They were lively and entertaining and good company. I was very proud of them.

Now that I'd had fifteen years of experience running a company, I felt like I had the best job in London publishing. We were, by then, sufficiently large enough to be able to publish whatever we wanted, assuming we could afford to make the right offer for it. I believed that the subjects of the books we were working on and the authors we were working with were really making a difference. We could see from the amount of review and feature coverage our books were receiving that there was a shift coming in society. Previously unmentionable topics at dinner parties – reincarnation, feng shui, counselling, therapies – were now being talked about openly. Sometimes people would tell us that reading some of the books we had published had changed their lives – and always in a good way.

It had become fashionable for companies of all sizes to create their own mission statements. Ours was along the lines of: "We publish books to entertain, to inform and to inspire." Individuals and organizations had not yet started to focus on their "purpose", but the topic was beginning to be written about in some of our self-help books. I had originally thought that my own purpose was simply to sell good books. But as the personal growth area began to expand and I read more books on the subject of how to think about my life, I realized that my purpose had become more about opening people's minds to new ways of thinking about the experiences they were having in their lives, both in their internal reflections and in the outer world around them. I realized that a person's purpose could change alongside them as they grew and developed. As the years passed and people grew older, there was often more time for contemplation about the meaning of their own life and what they felt about their roles, both in their family and the wider world, and an opportunity to reflect on the achievements for which they wanted to aim.

In the mid-1990s, a massive change rocked the publishing industry with the abolition of the Net Book Agreement. Until that time, publishers had been allowed to set the price of each book they published and that price had been non-negotiable. Now the agreement had been abolished, and retailers and publishers found themselves having to learn how to negotiate pricing and marketing deals with each other; overnight, publishers had lost control of their marketplace. There was one positive aspect to this change, though, because the new deal-making terrain allowed them to sell much higher volumes of certain books than ever before, although it was now the retailers who had the opportunity to decide what they wanted to promote and how they wanted to do it.

In 1991, Tim Waterstone launched his first bookshop in Kensington and after that there were regular new openings of Waterstones branches all over the country. There were several other bookshops chains – WHSmith was, at that time, the high street destination store; Dillons, whose huge flagship store was in Gower Street, just by London University; Ottakar's, and Hammicks. The huge American chain, Borders, launched in the UK during that period, with massive stores selling both books and records and offering relaxed informal cafés. Many independent bookstores were finding it hard to compete when one of the chain bookstores moved into their town. The book clubs were continuing to appeal to new readers and the German behemoth, Bertelsmann, also launched a new club, expanding the market for mail-order. Our books were ideal not only for the general book clubs but for the specialist business book clubs and the new mind, body, spirit book clubs.

We published so many exciting books on the Piatkus list in the 1990s. In spite of having no outside investment, we were able to grow our turnover slowly and steadily. We had, by then, published sufficient books during the preceding fifteen years that were still continuing to sell regularly, which gave us a sizeable backlist to which we were able to add. Even when business was slow, as it always was in some months, there was money coming in from books we had published years before. I would review the previous day's sales figures every morning when I came in and it was always one of the high points of my day – even in a slow month. I loved discovering unexpected wholesale and export orders that had arrived seemingly overnight. I liked the idea that our books were continuing to sell while I was asleep. At the end of the decade, when people had begun to use the internet, our morning review of the orders from the night before became even more exciting.

We could never tell which books we published would backlist. In our wildest dreams we never imagined the impact the first two books we bought from American author Jon Kabat-Zinn would have. Widely considered the founder of the present-day mindfulness movement, the first book of his to be offered to us was entitled *Wherever You Go, There You Are*. We weren't sure if people would know what the title meant (the topic of mindfulness was completely new to us too), so we changed it to *Mindfulness Meditation for Every Day*. The week it was published, the *Daily Mail* ran a huge feature and the first print run sold out almost immediately. Of course it has been in print ever since, becoming a classic. *Full Catastrophe Living*, Jon's first book and the next book of his that we published, was more than 700 pages long, an expensive investment and a huge leap of faith on our part. We never regretted our decision and, gradually, Jon's work on the practice of mindfulness began to be recommended by psychotherapists in the UK; and later, allied with the NHS, mindfulness clinics were set up to help people struggling with long-term pain management. Now, more than twenty years later, the practice of mindfulness has become part of mainstream culture.

Another American book that we were very excited to publish was *Many Lives, Many Masters* by Brian L. Weiss. This book had been out in the States for a couple of years when we came across it, and it was already a massive bestseller there and in South America. No one in the UK had wanted to take it on: possibly due to the fact that the memoir, which featured a highly-regarded doctor who accidentally came across a patient's ability to recall past-life traumas during therapy sessions, was deemed a bit too "out there" for British readers. I have lost count of the number of people who have recommended the book to me to read, not knowing that Piatkus first published it in the UK. For many, it has been life-changing, opening up their minds to a glimpse of mysterious unknown worlds. There was huge interest in reincarnation, near-death experiences and past-life regression during that decade.

One morning, during one of my annual American trips, I was waiting for an American colleague to join me for breakfast at Michael's, a smart Manhattan restaurant. I had arrived early and was amusing myself by watching the people at a round table for six nearby. Were they businesspeople or media, I wondered. The fifth person to arrive was a literary agent I had met a few times and now I focused more carefully on the people at the table. One man I thought I recognized from the photo on one of our book jackets and, plucking up courage, I went over to the group and spoke to the literary agent. He introduced me to his colleagues, three of them well-known authors of books on reincarnation, and for the first time I was able to meet and congratulate our own author, Dannion Brinkley, whose book *Saved by the Light*, about his own near-death experience, was currently at the top of the American bestseller list.

Denise Linn was one of our authors at that time. She had amassed a large following in different countries for her popular workshops. She came to London every year and put on marathon sessions in a large hall in Kensington, enabling several hundred people to experience past-life regression at the same time. I decided to attend one of these and persuaded Cyril, one of the most down-to-earth people you could imagine, to come with me. He was surprised how much he enjoyed the session. He saw himself in one of his previous lives as the captain of a pirate ship which had sailed around the seas in the Far East. No wonder he has always felt at home in that part of the world; his company was trading with the Far East, ordering products from Malaysia and Taiwan. Apparently, I was his favourite concubine in that life. We have laughed about it ever since.

Another book on reincarnation that was offered to us at that time – and which we were lucky to discover in the slush pile – became hugely influential for all those who were interested in the topic. Jenny Cockell was an Englishwoman who, from an early age, had very powerful memories of a previous life lived in Ireland where, as a young mother called Mary, she had experienced an early death, leaving several children behind.

After her funeral, the family was split up and the siblings lost touch with one another. Now in her late thirties – the age when she thought Mary had died – Jenny decided to visit Malahide, the place where Mary had lived in Ireland, to see if she could find the woman's family. There, she combed the local parish records, which led her to find a man she believed was her/Mary's oldest son, now in his sixties. Jenny was able to reveal to him things about his life with her that only his mother could have known. The subsequent publicity in Ireland enabled several of his siblings to be reunited with one another. Jenny's book, *Yesterday's Children*, received a huge amount of publicity in the UK and sold very well for us. It was subsequently published in America with a different title, *Across Time and Death*. We even sold an option to the film rights, although I am not sure if the film was ever made. For years afterwards, every time a television programme was made about reincarnation, Jenny was interviewed on it. Her story and that of the reunited family was considered as near to proof that reincarnation might be worth examining further as it was possible to find in the Western world.

Another ancient topic became hugely popular during this decade. Feng shui, also known as Chinese geomancy, is about arranging the placement of buildings and objects in such a way as to achieve the most harmony and balance possible in the space between them. Karen Kingston came to us with a book entitled *Creating Sacred Space with Feng Shui*. An Englishwoman living at that time in Bali and Australia, she was an expert on all aspects of the subject. Being prepared to take risks with new subjects, and being ahead of the publishing game in the UK, was what we were all about as a company. There was one chapter in Karen's book, on the subject of the clearing of clutter, which struck a particular chord with readers. It was to become the subject of Karen's next book for us, published in a small, square format with text and cover designed according to feng shui principles. *Clear Your Clutter with Feng Shui* turned out to be the most successful book that Piatkus initiated in my time as publisher. It has now sold millions of copies and been translated into many different languages. We sold American rights to Broadway, a fairly new Random House imprint; and we were very lucky when a major American chain of coffee shops, who were experimenting with selling books in their stores that year, then gave Broadway a substantial order for Karen's book. Although there have been many other bestsellers on the subject of decluttering since then, notably those by Japanese author Marie Kondo, Karen is without question the mother of the trend for space clearing in the home.

The Piatkus author whose work influenced me the most at the beginning of our journey into spiritual and esoteric publishing was Gill Edwards. She was an Englishwoman living in Highgate in London when we first met, before moving to the Lake District. She was very talented – a journalist, broadcaster and chartered clinical psychologist.

Sometimes we took a risk on a writer when we felt that what he or she was creating was so magical and life-expanding that we had a moral duty to put their work out there in the world. Gill Edwards was, for us, one of those special authors. I was sitting at home on one of my reading days when I read the first few chapters of her book, *Living Magically*, another of those very rare diamonds found in the slush pile. Gill wrote about the metaphysical world, about the relationship between mind and matter, the power of our thoughts to influence our lives, about the signs and symbols that are there for us to pay attention to, and the expanding of our consciousness. Everyone in the office loved Gill – we could feel what a beautiful, remarkable soul she was – but *Living Magically* was not an easy book to pitch to booksellers: a first-time author, especially one that wrote about mysticism, would be a hard sell. However, as Gill had a small but growing following from her regular spot on a local London radio station, we decided to take a chance on the book.

Gill offered to come to the office and give us a sample of one of her workshops. We sat in a large circle in our reception area and she took us through a guided meditation and visualization, an experience that was a first for most of us. Gill's mellifluous voice took us on a journey in our minds and at the end of the meditation we were told to envisage receiving a special gift. Mine turned out to be a beautiful book with a golden cover that sparkled in the light. I still remember the feeling I experienced when I saw that incredible book in my mind. *What a perfect gift*, I thought. I can still see it now.

Sadly Gill Edwards died in 2011, but her mind-expanding books – especially *Living Magically* and *Stepping into the Magic* – influenced thousands of people. We were so privileged to have known her and to have been able to play a part in making her inspiring ideas about how we live available to the world.

TWENTY TWO
THE MIND–BODY CONNECTION

People had gradually begun to explore complementary therapies in the 1980s. Initially, the term used was "alternative" remedies, and there was a certain amount of distrust, even hostility toward them from the more conservative members of the medical profession – and, indeed, society. Once again, Piatkus, came to these subjects with an interested and open mind; the fact that we published books on so many of what were, back then, distinctly niche subjects, standing us in good stead.

Our medical system in the West is not set up to look at our bodies and our minds holistically, an attitude and training that contrasts strongly with the East, where the body is viewed as an energy system. It was becoming clear that even the kindest and most diligent doctors were not able to heal everyone and that some illnesses go beyond the bounds of traditional medicine. We published books on reflexology, aromatherapy, shiatsu, tai chi, qigong, meditation and the Alexander Technique in the 1980s; so ahead of the times that we first had to explain what these therapies were to our sales force, who, in turn, would have to make these unknown therapies intelligible to the book buyers. Gradually, as journalists started to write features about these treatments and practices, the public wanted to know more.

The ground-breaking bestseller that had inspired so many people to think about the mind–body connection was Louise Hay's *You Can Heal Your Life* (which was published in America by her own company, Hay House). This led to other books, and we published one of my all-time favourites: *Your Body Speaks Your Mind* by Deb Shapiro. Whenever anyone in my family is ill, this is always the first book I consult, wanting always to understand the emotional cause of an illness so that I can think about how both the mind and the body can work together to heal.

We also published a number of books about improving your sex life. The 1990s was a more carefree time, and there was a focus on having fun and enjoying yourself. Alex Comfort's massive bestseller, *The Joy of Sex*, broke new ground in this area, and our titles – including *Becoming Orgasmic*, *What Makes a Woman Sexy*, *How to be a Great Lover* and Margot Anand's classic book on Tantric sex, *The Art of Sexual Magic* – sold very well for us. We tried to find a new sex title every season as they were so popular with the book clubs and with WHSmith. I remember going into one of the larger branches one day and counting over fifty different sex-related titles on display. The only downside for me was that none of my editorial colleagues would want to pitch the books at sales meetings and conferences, so it was usually left to me to stand up and enthuse. Once again we published with the times, catching every new wave of interest. Research indicates that people these days aren't enjoying or giving time to their sex lives in the way they did in the 1990s; working long hours and allowing our leisure time to be eaten up by digital devices and hours of box-set viewing have had a deleterious effect.

In the middle of the 1990s, we had a very quiet and thoughtful editor, Heather Rocklin. Before she left to go on maternity leave, she acquired books by two very different authors, both of whose body of work was to become very influential. Jane Scrivner, who founded the British School of Complementary Therapy, was an inspiring natural writer who approached us directly because she liked our books. Her first book for us was *Detox Yourself:*

Feel the Benefits After Only 7 Days. The book was possibly the first commercial mass-market paperback on the topic and after we published in January 1998, with an initial order of 3,000 copies from WHSmith for their New Year health promotion, it went on to sell 100,000 copies and started the massive trend for detoxing. Jane wrote further books for us which also did well, including *Detox Your Mind* and a tiny, square book entitled *The Little Book of Detox*, which sold in its thousands. "Little books" were very popular at this time as gifts and impulse purchases – and they were also fun to publish. However, online selling has made them almost obsolete, as thumbnail cover photographs on the screen cannot really do them justice.

The other author who Heather introduced to us was Patrick Holford. His first book for us, *The Optimum Nutrition Bible*, came out the same season as *Detox Yourself.* It was to become a gold standard of our backlist as, after it became established, this magnum opus began to sell upwards of 2,000 copies for us every month. I credit Patrick for raising awareness of nutrition and the English diet in a way that had not really been done before. He had, at that time, founded the Institute of Optimum Nutrition and was training nutritionists in his way of thinking. His work sparked off huge public discourse about the nature of the food we eat, drawing attention to the impact of our diet on our overall health and wellbeing. If only more people would heed the message.

Gradually the influence of Patrick's ideas spread across the world. With Gill's editorial guidance, he wrote many more books, in particular a further classic text, *Optimum Nutrition for the Mind*, and a number of other valuable titles about different aspects of nutrition. Patrick's books were particularly successful in South Africa and Australia, both countries that he visited regularly, where Philip worked closely with our distributors and with Patrick to build his profile as an expert and bestselling author. Several times he was able to occupy the number one non-fiction bestseller slot for his work in those markets, and for the next twenty years barely a publishing season went by without a new and noteworthy book from him. Patrick has always been an amazing innovator, keen to explore new ideas and forever pushing at the boundaries of what people are interested to learn about – the perfect partner for an innovative entrepreneurial outfit such as ours. Whenever he walked into the room, I would feel myself automatically sitting up straight. His energy was always infectious in the best possible way.

There was one more book which we published in that decade which has always held pride of place on my bookshelf. *Women's Bodies, Women's Wisdom* by Dr Christiane Northrup was a huge American tome about women's health. The health system is very different in America from the British NHS, but the topic of women's bodies is universal. The book was 900 pages long, but Gill and I felt it was such an important title that it would be worthwhile engaging in the huge task of going through every page and anglicizing the text – something we rarely needed to do with American books – to make it suitable for the British market. It was a massive undertaking, as we had to change so much terminology and employ an expert to check that everything we had written was accurate for the UK market and for our key export markets.

The book was published in 1998. Christiane Northrup came to the UK to promote it on publication and was absolutely charming. One morning, I came into the office to find that, unexpectedly, hundreds of orders had come in overnight and we had virtually sold out of our first printing. It took us a while to track down what had caused the excitement about the book. Eventually we discovered that Christiane, who was Oprah's Winfrey's gynaecologist, had been interviewed on the American presenter's television programme – and the programme had been shown on an afternoon television channel in the UK. The orders department in the warehouse was going ballistic with requests. It was thrilling and we felt it was justly deserved, both for it being such a good book and for our hard work and commitment to it. *Women's Bodies, Women's Wisdom* went on to sell over 100,000 copies in our edition. It has made a major contribution to women's understanding of how their physical and emotional health and wellbeing are all inter-connected. When people used to ask me which of my books I was proudest to have published, this was always one of the titles in the forefront of my mind.

TWENTY THREE
CONQUERING THE MASS MARKET

After our failed attempt at mass-market paperback fiction publishing, with our ugly pink and yellow paperback covers, it took me a few years to want to put my toe back in the water. It was the only way we would be able to compete for better books, however. The trouble was that the sums of money involved posed a much greater risk for us than for many other independent publishers, most of whom published more serious literary fiction. Our authors, with very few exceptions, were wholly commercial; our major customers, if we were to launch paperbacks, would be WHSmith in high streets and airports, and the supermarkets, the biggest markets for paperback novels at that time. That meant we would be competing for space with all the famous publishing houses who launched major authors with a sizeable marketing budget every month.

It is much harder to find a promotional angle for a novelist than it is for a non-fiction book, so it is always a challenge to find a way to persuade bookshops to give a new novelist some shelf space unless they have a local connection. We would have to work very hard to create a new brand and carve out a niche for ourselves. We couldn't afford to get our paperback list wrong a second time, so we briefed freelance designers who had worked for other paperback houses; and our UK sales director, Diane, showed the covers to the buyers at a very early stage to make sure we had got them right. We determined to launch the list slowly but thoughtfully and were expecting to make mistakes – from which we knew we needed to learn as quickly as we could.

Our first few titles were genre fiction – sagas, crime and romances. Following the success of Catherine Cookson's novels, sagas had become hugely popular in the 1990s. The heroine of each saga was usually a woman from a poor background who was finally able to overcome her difficult early years and find a handsome and kind lover with whom she could live happily ever after – if she didn't die in childbirth first, of course, thereby creating what became known as a "weepie". Sagas were usually set in specific regions – Scotland, Ireland, Cornwall, the North East of England and London's East End were particularly popular. (For some reason Wales and the Midlands didn't do so well!)

We soon learned how to publish these quite successfully and many of our authors' sales began to grow. This made us more confident to publish a much wider range of interesting women writers. The popular women's fiction category known as "Aga sagas" were all the rage by then, a trend led by the author Joanna Trollope. The book covers for this "middle England" genre featured illustrations rather than photographs, and the designs were very distinctive, epitomizing a certain kind of cosy English lifestyle.

After a few years, our fiction paperback list had begun to build a reputation for publishing good quality commercial writers, whose work would appeal to women of all ages who enjoyed a well-written story. Most of our books could not be considered literary or highbrow, but occasionally an author came to us who was more serious, and thus we were able to add novels by Marge Piercy, Shifra Horn and Lynne Reid Banks to our list. We also published crime fiction, although that was much more of a challenge as, at that time, it was easier to sell crime and thrillers by authors with a considerable track record. Our crime fiction was therefore much more tentative and we relied mostly on American thriller writers with a previous track record, which helped us in the library and export markets.

In fiction, as in all other markets, tastes are constantly changing and soon the sagas were overtaken by a new genre inspired by a massive bestseller, *Bridget Jones's Diary* by Helen Fielding. These books, which became known as "chick lit", were frequently written for a younger age group and focused on humorous, heroine-centred narratives. In 1997, an experienced author came to us with an idea for a chick lit novel she would write under the pseudonym Zoe Barnes. Her first novel for us, *Bumps*, was packaged with the strapline "Sexy, single, successful ... and pregnant". Zoe Barnes had a deliciously light and comic touch and the book was absolutely on trend.

We were so excited about the sales potential for *Bumps* that we planned tube advertising, national and regional press ads and a publicity campaign for the author. Happily, the supermarkets loved the book and everything we were planning to do to market it, and supported us in a major way. It became our first paperback bestseller, reaching the UK top ten in the week of publication and going on to sell 60,000 copies. We were all thrilled to bits, while at the same time heaving a huge sigh of relief. We had gambled a lot of money on its success. Fortunately, the export markets liked the package and did well with the book too.

Zoe, whose real name was Susan Morgan, followed it up a year later with a novel called *Hitched*, about a bride who wasn't sure she wanted to get married. The following year we published *Hot Property*, about a couple trying to buy their first home. The idea for this had come from our in-house editorial team, all of whose friends were trying to get onto the property ladder. By then, the Zoe Barnes brand had built up huge momentum and our first printing for this third book was a massive 95,000 copies. We had solid orders but it was still pretty nerve-racking as we needed the books to sell through and not be returned. In the event, *Hot Property* did sell very well and the returns weren't too high. Although we were never to achieve that number again for a single first printing, I didn't mind, knowing we couldn't afford to go out on such a limb very often. The main thing was that we knew we could now consider ourselves a fully-fledged paperback publisher. We had arrived.

As books in the UK are usually sold to shops and stores on a sale-or-return basis, no matter who your customer is or how many copies they are ordering, every retailer will have the right to return them. If the books come back damaged, it is the publisher who takes the hit, never wishing to have an argument with a major corporate client. When we entered the paperback market, we had to think each month about the allocation of financial reserves to cover this; high returns could impact severely on our cash flow. The supermarkets and WHSmith would order large quantities to distribute to each of their branches and, after their time on display, we knew we would get several thousands of books back, few of which we could sell on to another customer. "You pay to play," I would say to myself, gritting my teeth as I gave the order to pulp the copies and write off some of the profit. We wanted to be successful but it always came at a price.

TWENTY FOUR

MY NEW SIDELINE

Sometimes I have thought that, just like BC and AD, we need some initials to denote the period before the technological age began. The early part of the 1990s was such a different time from the latter half of the decade, as technology in the form of computers slowly encroached on all our lives, both at home and at work. Before that time, even though I was running a sizeable company and always had a large pile of reading to do, I felt that my evenings were my own and I do think it was much easier for executive working mothers.

Every morning, I would get up at six-thirty to write my morning pages for twenty-five minutes before catching the tube to the office. "Morning pages" were the creation of American author Julia Cameron, whose million-copy bestseller *The Artist's Way* (sadly not offered to us to publish) has had a huge impact on my life. Offering the reader a twelve-week course in creativity, Julia believed that the act of writing three pages in longhand every morning was immensely valuable. Indeed, I found it improved my creativity and productivity immensely. I would write about whatever came into my head and, after a while, those things that needed to take precedence in the workplace came bubbling up in my thinking. I would go to the computer and send the relevant emails or take other actions as necessary, and, by the time I arrived in the office at eight-thirty, I had a clear sense of what was going on and what I needed to focus on during that day. I also found that it helped me come up with new ideas. Morning pages are a truly remarkable workplace tool. Later on, I was to realize that, for me, my morning pages were a form of writing meditation. It was a habit I would continue for many years to come.

Although always aware of my responsibilities to my colleagues and authors, I also felt much freer before the advent of the computer or smart phone. We did not have an office culture of being in touch after we had left the office for the evening or the weekend, so there was a very clear demarcation between the world of work and the world outside of it.

On the tube into work, I usually read part of a typescript or an early bound proof copy of an American book we had been offered for publication and I would always pop out for a lunch break to get fresh air and fresh food – often a salad from Cranks or Planet Organic (after all, we did publish health books). In the office, if people wanted to speak to me, they rang me on the internal phone system, and, though my in-tray was always piled high with memos, faxes and other reading material, I wouldn't have the panicky sight of hundreds of new emails greeting me each day. Instead, throughout my day, I would have face-to-face meetings and conversations. I've mentioned earlier how the publishing industry is all about relationships. Even after large expense accounts had become a thing of the past in many industries, publishers continued to take authors and agents out to lunch. I would leave the office at about five-thirty and be home an hour later to have dinner with my family. Our family time was always sacrosanct to me and I only made evening exceptions when there was a publishing reception to go to, or when the occasional author came to London from abroad and my attendance at dinner was required. After supper, I would usually read for an hour or two until I got too tired. It was a very satisfying way of life.

As my children grew older and became more self-sufficient, and as we published more self-help books, there grew in me a yearning for something beyond the world of publishing. Being a natural creative, I realized that I needed to create something new and different in my personal life. I was giving out energy all day, every day to other people and, while I was happy to do this, I felt that there was a want and a need in me for something more for myself. Just what that "something" might be was hard to understand, because I had thought that I already did have everything I needed to be happy.

I wasn't drawn to charity work as I found it difficult to ask for money from friends; and because I sat in meetings all day in the office, I didn't want to take part in more meetings in my free time. I had tried yoga on a couple of different occasions in the 1980s and didn't love it. When we had to lie on the floor of a draughty church hall to relax at the end of the session, I usually fell asleep and I didn't enjoy having to wake up, get dressed, go home and get undressed again before falling into bed. I also didn't want to entertain friends during the week – that was too much like hard work – nor did I have the energy to go to the theatre much. All the early mornings and the massive amount of reading I had to do often made me tired.

One day, a friend invited me to her home for a charity event she was hosting. A dynamic woman had been invited to address the meeting and tell us about the telephone helpline she ran. Miyad, the helpline that I decided to get involved with, was unlike the Samaritans because it was not limited to those who were thinking suicidal thoughts or feeling suicidal. As a result, we were not restricted to a more structured approach in our conversations with people. Much to my surprise, I had found that extra something that I had been looking for to fulfil my personal life. I thought I might enjoy talking anonymously to people of different backgrounds and I volunteered for the six-week training course. This was to be my first experience of learning the rudiments of how to listen well, a skill which I was also able to make good use of in the office. I learned the art of "mirroring": acknowledging people's words by repeating them so that they knew I had heard what they were saying and would hopefully be encouraged to continue talking to me. Paraphrasing was another skill I acquired, learning to sum up the essence of what someone might have spent several minutes unloading onto me and repeating it succinctly back to them to confirm that I had understood. In the training groups we role-played and practised until, finally, we were allowed to sit by the phone.

There was no time limit on each call and some of them lasted as long as an hour. We spoke with men and women contemplating divorce, or who were grieving; young girls who had miscarried; older men who were lonely; gay men who had not been able to come out; trans men and women who had not been able to speak out. The list of relationship challenges for human beings is endless. Some stories were heartbreaking, and I was glad there was always an experienced on-duty supervisor whom the volunteers could call if they needed to talk through a very difficult conversation.

I had spent my life reading a huge variety of fiction genres. I had reflected on so many different kinds of human situation. Yet here was the pain of life in the raw. It was a massive contrast to the way I spent my days in the office. My shift at the helpline was from nine in the evening until midnight. I would reflect on many of the people I spoke with and the lives they lived as I drove home along the dark, empty motorway. It was rewarding and meaningful work, and I felt extremely privileged that so many people were prepared to open up to me about their most intimate secrets. I was also loving the sharp contrast with publishing. It was very relaxing after a day in the office to think about other people from completely different backgrounds to mine and with completely different expectations of how their lives should be.

After a couple of years on the helpline, I decided that I could offer more help to people if I had further training. I also thought I would enjoy having a relationship with one person for a longer amount of time. I wondered what it would be like to experience an ongoing relationship with a client, meeting face to face. The opportunity arose to join a bereavement counselling service and I applied and was accepted. Sixteen of us started at the same time, mainly women, but after a couple of years only four of us were left from the original group. The bereavement counselling involved going to people's homes to be with them for an hour. I would have one client at a time and go to see them once a week, usually for continuing sessions of up to twelve weeks.

Every day, people lose loved ones and emerge through their tunnel of grief onto the other side. But there are always people whose grief is so enormous that they feel unable to manage it with only the support of their friends and families. They need a space that is just for them, where they can express themselves in any way they want, say anything they want, and feel free not to hold back. Bereavement counselling is a hugely valuable service, which is not often appreciated until you are the person who is needing it. Sometimes families, exhausted with trying to cope, referred grieving relatives because they didn't know how to be with them any longer.

But what was particularly interesting about working with deep loss was how often the presenting loss – the one that we heard about first, the reason why the client felt they needed to speak to us – was not in fact the true cause of the grief. So many of us experience unmourned loss in our lives. We may lose family members when they are tiny babies or children; we may lose beloved grandparents, older siblings, special friends or mentors. We might even need to mourn a childhood home or a beloved pet. So often the grief of those losses was not recognized or sufficiently acknowledged at the time of the loss. When one parent dies, supporting the living parent may mean there is not sufficient time to grieve the lost one. It is only when the second parent dies that the grief can feel like a much more painful blow. Frequently, it needs an expert counsellor to delve beneath the surface to gently ease out the hidden stories of unmourned loss. As bereavement counsellors, we were always gently digging, looking for the real reason why our clients' grief was so overwhelming that they had been unable to cope on their own. At Piatkus, we had begun to publish more books about emotions and feelings; now I was experiencing them in the raw. It was a profound learning experience.

TWENTY FIVE

THE 49-YEAR-OLD STUDENT

I worked with the bereavement organization one evening a week for more than two years. Increasingly, over that time, I began to feel that if I had more training, I would be able to help clients more effectively, because I would understand better what was happening during our time together. I was curious. What would it really be like to become a trained counsellor? When I enquired where I could go to learn more basic skills and techniques, I was recommended to try Regent's College, a private establishment in Central London which had a highly-regarded counselling and psychotherapy faculty. I applied for the Introduction to Counselling course, which I would attend on a Monday evening after work. It would be tough; alongside all the new reading I would be given, I also had my regular mountain of typescripts from work.

There were twenty-five students in the class, of varying ages and backgrounds. One of the first things you have to work at when you become a counsellor, whether voluntary or otherwise, is to be non-judgemental of others. On the first evening, we started off all sitting in a large circle and introducing ourselves. I didn't feel judgemental at all. I was so thrilled to be there. Finally, at the age of forty-nine, I was a student again, sitting in a classroom, ready to learn new skills that would eventually lead to a qualification, even though it might only be a very basic one. It was more than thirty years since I had failed to get the university place I'd wanted. Being on this course – in the middle of my life – felt like a huge achievement. At last I had found something I really wanted to learn which, unexpectedly, might even lead to a real paper qualification to hang on my wall at home.

We learned about different theories of counselling: psychodynamic, which is based on Freudian ideas; existential, about the meaning of life; and humanistic, a completely non-judgemental approach to all human beings developed by Carl Rogers. We also explored a wide range of different topics that might arise in the counselling room. One of the lectures that impacted me strongly was on gender, a subject that I knew, on one level, I had spent my life avoiding discussing. As the lecture progressed, I was shocked into recognizing that I had been in denial about issues around my own gender and being a woman in business for the whole of my career. Throughout the last twenty-five years, I had coped with being a working woman by ignoring the topic and staying completely focused on my business goals. I had wanted to publish a range of books that sold and I wanted some of the books among the range to empower women. We had published very many books that improved women's lives, and we had been on a mission to enable women to have more confidence in themselves so they could go forward and achieve their dreams, ambitions and goals. We wanted them to be treated equally and to be able to hold their own wherever they went. We wanted them to look good and feel good about themselves. No opportunity had previously arisen, however, to question my own inner beliefs and thinking on the topic. I realized I had a lot of self-exploration to do.

I had never regarded myself as a feminist. The feminist publishers were doing great work, but it was more my own personal style to be quietly assertive and collaborative with everyone who wanted to work with us. I didn't want to be seen by men as "other", simply wanting to be treated as and regarded by them as an equal. I didn't need people to like me, but I did want to be respected for the quality of my work, in the way Piatkus needed to be respected for the quality of its books and the professionalism with which we produced, marketed and sold them. Foremost in my mind was always the knowledge that I was not prepared to be considered a second-class citizen by anyone.

In later years, I would often reflect just how much my gender and the ideas of my female colleagues had impacted on the way we had built the company. But that evening, in that classroom, I experienced quite a reckoning with myself.

For several years now, I had been a member of the International Women's Forum, the networking organization for senior women executives. We still met monthly for breakfast at the Ritz Hotel in Piccadilly and interesting evening events were regularly arranged by us. I found it very helpful to listen to other senior – and frequently distinguished – female leaders talking about their experiences. Most of them worked for corporations or in the public sector, and the conversation was usually more about new trends in business thinking and company management. I didn't remember ever having conversations about gender or the sexual power balance. In my experience, women who grew up in the 1950s tend to speak to one another with much less sharing of detailed intimacies than younger women do nowadays. It was a much less open time.

A few weeks after the lecture, I spoke with a few other women at the Forum about what I had learned. Those women of my age and older with whom I spoke recognized that they too had operated like me. It was so hard to succeed as a woman in business or the public sector in the 1980s that each one of us had felt that we'd had to put all thoughts of our gender aside and simply concentrate on the task in hand. We rarely ever spoke about our personal lives, our families or our children if we had them. Our focus, will and persistence had pushed and pulled us towards our goals. We had worked very hard to be treated as equals through our competence and professional skills.

None of us had ever asked for any special treatment because we were women, and sometimes mothers and carers. All of us had felt that if we were to do that, it would have been seen as a sign of weakness. In order to reach the top of our organizations, whether in public or private, we had unconsciously obliterated all those parts of ourselves that might have got in the way of our goals and ambitions. This didn't necessarily mean that we had tried to behave like men in the workplace. Each one of us had had to find our own path to the top in a period of history with few role models. It had probably been easier for me, being my own boss and working in publishing, an industry where there were many outstanding and respected women, albeit not always in the most senior positions.

After the year's introductory counselling course ended, my fellow students and I were offered the option of studying for diplomas in either psychodynamic psychotherapy or in existential counselling. I couldn't bear to give up my newfound joy in serious learning and was determined to find a way to carry on. Psychodynamic psychotherapy appealed to me because it explored childhood influences and the counsellor worked with the client's unconscious mind. The Diploma in Psychodynamic Psychotherapy and Counselling was a two-year course. Students had to attend classes for three terms each year, from two till nine, one day a week. In addition, we would have to find ourselves a placement in an organization where we could practise our new counselling skills. We were also required to pay for personal therapy, a minimum of forty-two sessions. How could we possibly counsel and work with others if we hadn't been in therapy ourselves? If we did not understand our own background and influences, including those wrought on our later lives by our family of origin, we could find ourselves drawn into other people's lives in an inappropriate way. Learning about ourselves would help all of us understand ourselves better and enable us to work with clients in a detached way.

There were fewer students on this course and several dropped out during the first few months. It was very challenging, and included lectures, skills tuition, role-play, essay writing and group therapy. Many of my fellow students had been in therapy before; some of them had lived such difficult lives. A lot of deep pain was to be shared.

I am not sure exactly what I learned about myself at that time, but I did learn a lot about other people. Deep listening enables you to hear what other people are saying at a more profound level. It encourages more enquiry. I found that my relationships with many people could be more intimate as a result. We were able to engage in conversation at a much more significant level than I had previously been used to and we could often reach that level very quickly. As a result, my exchanges and interactions with clients and my fellow students became much more meaningful. I had to be careful not to bring too much of that into the office though, as it was always important to establish and maintain very clear boundaries between all of us. As a leader, I needed to set a good example of that.

I hadn't talked much with my colleagues at Piatkus about the introductory course I had taken on Monday nights. There had been no need to do so. But now I was planning further studies, I definitely had to come clean. I announced that I would be taking off a half day each week, saying, "If I were a man I would probably tell you I was going to play golf." To take time out from being in the office, simply to improve myself, was very unusual in the commercial world at that time. It was before life coaching had become a phenomenon (and shortly afterwards we did have great success in 1999 with one of the first books on this topic, Eileen Mulligan's *Life Coaching: Change Your Life in 7 Days*). I had been working without a real break since the age of nineteen. Surely I could take some time out? I told myself and my colleagues that my new skills would, of course, benefit the company.

Continuing to study felt like pure indulgence and I couldn't entirely make sense of it: I had a wonderful and interesting career, which I loved, but I knew – with every fibre of my being –

that I had to continue to learn more about psychotherapy. I had always been so responsible about everything connected with my business. Now, managing to persuade myself that I wouldn't let anyone down, that I would continue with my high standards of working, I followed my desires and intuition that all would work out, and enrolled. Just what my colleagues were making of this I didn't dare to enquire. I told them I would continue to do my work as before, reassuring them nothing would change and that I would be at my desk as usual every other day of the week.

My husband was, as always, very supportive. What could possibly go wrong?

TWENTY SIX
TURN OF THE CENTURY

My two and a half years of studying to be a counsellor had finally come to an end. I was very proud of my achievement in gaining a Diploma in Psychodynamic Psychotherapy and Counselling. It was an amazing experience to wear a gown and graduate as a mature student. I was now in my early fifties. Completely committed to the task, I had studied hard and had worked for over 450 hours in a doctor's practice in London's West End. I had counselled people of all ages, from different countries and backgrounds and with a wide variety of challenging issues. I hoped that I had become more compassionate and had greater understanding of how very hard some people's lives could be – and how there are always so many heroes and heroines amongst us, courageous in situations that many of us cannot imagine ever having to face.

"When the student is ready, the teacher appears" had once again been an apposite saying for me. I had been ready for a new challenge. My teacher had come in the form of my college course, the interesting relationships I had entered into with my fellow students and with clients – and subsequently a new relationship with myself. I could have continued to work privately. But by then I had also realized that it wouldn't be possible to build a successful career in counselling and psychotherapy and be a publisher at the same time. My certificate hung in a frame on the wall over my desk at home. Now it was time to turn my full attention back to the world of books.

Of course the company had suffered while I distracted myself with other people and places for part of each week. My colleagues were professionals and all of us had continued to do our jobs, but they knew – as I did – that I hadn't been giving 100 percent to the business. In most people's careers there are times when other aspects of our lives take over. I had told myself that I wasn't indispensable; anyway, if there was a crisis, the college was just up the road from the office and I could call a cab and be back there very quickly if I was needed.

Now fully back in the saddle, I could see that the company and I were at a crossroads. Business was very tough and we had recently lost a large sum of money when one of our key export customers had to close down. I loved being a publisher but knew that if I were unable to work for myself, it was doubtful I could hold down a job for long working for someone else. When I made mistakes I didn't want to have to defend myself to anyone except my colleagues. When I did make errors – and there were plenty of them – I gave myself a hard time until I had learned from my mistakes. I didn't want a boss, bank manager or outside shareholders telling me what to do and how to think. I had enjoyed too many years of freedom. But, right now, the spectre of failure was ever present.

Over the years, we had seen many publishing companies fail and many small companies survive, living from hand to mouth. Entry barriers to publishing have traditionally been low, because no qualifications are required to publish and sell books. But remaining in business for many years and consistently producing quality books to sell in sufficient quantities each season, so that the profit generated would pay for the next season's books – all this required a cool head and nerves of steel. Or other people's money – but that had always been a route I didn't want to take. I also understood that even if the business did grow, I wanted to continue to enjoy myself coming to work each day. I loved the challenge of running an efficient, profitable company, but the increase of bureaucracy over the years meant that if I wasn't careful I would be spending my time doing tasks I didn't enjoy. I couldn't see the point of growing too big if I didn't have time to be close to the books I was helping to nurture. The problem now was: where next? I didn't have a clear vision for the future; the new century was about to begin and we needed a radical rethink.

By the year 2000, bookshop shelves were heaving with hundreds of self-help, how-to, motivational, personal development and all manner of spiritual titles. All of the large publishers were competing with one another to get into this area, publishing huge numbers of books in these categories. Some days we felt completely swamped by the competition. As an innovative publishing company, we had always prided ourselves on being at the leading edge. Now we were struggling to find authors with new and exciting things to say. We continued to publish good work by authoritative experts, but these weren't turning into books that would have a long life because there was too much competition. At the same time, the internet was changing the commercial world that we were used to – and it was all happening very fast. It was becoming quite worrying.

Three years earlier, we had called in a management consultant to review the company for the second time in our history. He had recommended that we needed to install our first computer system. We took his advice and hired a small company to create our first network. The project was expensive but, once we had received our initial training sessions and each of us had had a chance to play with our new toy, we all began to get used to this new method of communicating with each other and with those companies and authors who had already installed their own computers. It still took quite a while to get used to emailing people when we were working in the same room with them. Nowadays, no one would give it a second thought.

Computerizing the company coincided with a new customer arriving on the block. At the time, no one – not even Jeff Bezos himself, the CEO of Amazon – could have known how online retailing would disrupt so many industries in so many different ways or how it would become the forerunner of a whole new world of global commerce. Amazon approached UK publishing companies and ordered one or two copies of every book in print for their warehouse shelves as demand for their online offering built. It was to be the beginning of the end for so many small independent retailers and some of the larger chains, too, but few people recognized it at the time.

We had reinvented Piatkus at the start of the recession ten years previously, opening up new publishing opportunities for ourselves. As the new millennium dawned, our programme still maintained its cutting-edge status, with more books about coaching and NLP (neuro-linguistic programming) – the new kid on the block in the personal development area – as well as a green handbook published ahead of its time, *Eco Living* by Karen Christensen. But our overheads had increased considerably. As our staff had multiplied, we'd had to build an extra floor on our Windmill Street building and half of the editorial department had moved up there (getting fitter by the day, as they were now five floors up from the basement and our building did not have a lift). Even with that new space, there was still not quite enough room and, eventually, we were able to rent the ground floor of a building on the other side of the street, where the sales and publicity departments had moved in.

By now we were publishing a lot of books, about eighty a year. In addition, there was always a large number of reprints every month, which had to be scheduled – and paid for. Our turnover at that time was between £5,000,000 and £6,000,000, and if we needed to grow we would need to think about acquiring another business. Because publishing is so labour-intensive and because the price of most of our books was under £10, I thought it would be impossible to achieve otherwise. We had occasionally been offered small companies that we might have been able to afford but none had felt quite right. Although we liked the idea of a new adventure, we also knew that were we to acquire another company we would have to pay for new premises to house staff and that it would take a while for the company's culture to bed down with ours.

In one of the many business books we published, I remember reading that fewer than 20 percent of entrepreneur-led companies are still independently owned after fourteen years. We had now been in existence for more than twenty. Over the years, people had sidled up to me occasionally at publishing parties and invited me to "come and have a chat" if I ever wanted to sell. But I was still enjoying my work and wasn't ready for that.

But I also knew we needed to find a way to reinvent the company once again, now that our specialist area of the market had become so overcrowded. We didn't want to buy a company; I didn't want to sell my company. What could we do? Unexpectedly, the answer would be provided courtesy of Amazon.

TWENTY SEVEN

THE FIVE-YEAR PLAN

We needed a plan, a new direction and we needed the right specialist help in coming up with it. A senior executive coach, with whom I had had a few sessions, recommended me to the turnaround division of a large and well-known company of accountants. It was the third time we were to hire external consultants, but this was to be a much more expensive exercise. One of my challenges in my years as an entrepreneur had always been that I rarely had the opportunity to speak to interesting businesspeople working in different industries, aside from the women I met at the Forum network. Sometimes I would overhear my husband having interesting conversations at social events, but I was usually expected to talk to people's wives. In spite of all the people I now knew in the publishing industry, it was still difficult to have the conversations I wanted and needed about how best to run a business of our size.

Now I was to meet with two dynamic guys in their forties who had huge knowledge of all kinds of businesses. During their careers, they had met with very many different types of entrepreneur. Hopefully, they would be able to see and appreciate all that we had achieved, as well as what we hadn't got right. I prayed that, at last, I had found people to whom I could really talk about the company. I wanted to let down my defences and have an honest conversation with professionals who could help me.

First, the consultants said, I would have to look at myself: my strengths and weaknesses and what I wanted for my future. They asked me questions about my home life. How did I see myself living in five years' time? When might I want to stop working? Did I have any other ambitions that I wanted to realize? What kind of life might I want to lead in the future? Did I want more material rewards, such as a second home where I could retire at weekends? What were my hobbies and interests?

I didn't know what I wanted my future life to look like, but I did know that I didn't want to be walking the aisles of the Frankfurt Book Fair after the age of sixty. I was in my very early fifties, my key colleagues a few years older. However much we enjoyed our working time together, our close-knit team couldn't carry on for ever. I loved the world of publishing, books and authors – but I knew there was a world outside of it that I wanted time to explore. I wanted to travel, meet people, have new experiences – and to do that while I was young and fit enough.

I came to the conclusion that I would want to sell the company in a few years' time. We looked at the turnover and what the company would need to achieve so that I wouldn't have to worry about money in the future. I decided that the time for me to go would be when we had achieved a profitable turnover of £10,000,000. If we managed it, it would be a notable achievement as the company turnover was only a little more than half that sum at present. But why not give it our best shot? There was everything to play for and nothing to lose.

The next question to explore was how we might achieve this beautiful goal. The two management consultants said I needed to form a board of directors. Who would I like to join me in this enterprise? I named Philip and Gill, Diane, Simon, our financial manager at the time, and Gillian Green, who had joined us fairly recently from Mills and Boon and was proving particularly adept at buying good commercial fiction. The group was invited to come together for a two-day workshop with the consultants, which turned out to be a very stormy experience. In order to look at where we wanted to be, we had to start by looking at all the things that hadn't been working very well.

For three years now, I had been physically present in the office, but my head had often been elsewhere. I was tired from all the extra hours of studying for my diploma and often found myself deep in thought – not about my work at Piatkus but about the people I was counselling. In our workshop, I was prepared to face up to the damage I might have caused and I felt confident that good things would come out of it all.

After the weaknesses of and threats to the business had been discussed, we needed to look at our strengths as individuals and as a team, and our opportunities. We were an experienced, stable unit, and with so much talent between us I felt confident we would find a strategy that was right for the times. Happily, I felt we were all going in the same direction: the group loved the idea of aiming for a £10,000,000 turnover goal in five years. They understood that were we to reach it, we might be able to build cash reserves in the bank and would not be firefighting all the time. Our major challenge was going to be what to publish and how to reinvent ourselves for the twenty-first century.

Our business book range had become out of date almost overnight because of the recent changes in technology. Our personal growth list was still very solid, but we were finding it difficult to help authors develop big brands. Mind, body, spirit authors were coming to us with good books, but often they only had one book in them. It requires a hugely creative mind to keep coming up with fresh commercial ideas; authors who can do that for a publishing company are like gold dust. While we had to accept that non-fiction was getting harder to publish, we also realized that we were building a list of novelists who were able to deliver good books every year. Now that the online purchasing of books through Amazon was beginning to grow, we would be able to reach our readers much more easily. If their local bookshop didn't stock their favourite author, we could reach our audience online.

The new team went away feeling encouraged but also apprehensive. We hadn't worked together as a group of directors before and to do so would require discipline. Would we be able to do it? We had been advised to hold our monthly board meetings away from the office and we found a small private room in a hotel in Charlotte Street. We only booked it for two hours, so everyone knew that we would have to use the time well. Simon would take the minutes, and we would start by reviewing those of the last meeting, share what was happening in each of our areas and plan for the future.

Gradually, we could see that this new disciplined way of working was beginning to bear fruit. There was one problem, though. Our financial manager did not seem completely comfortable with aspects of the new system, so we then hired Preeya Modessa, a young and enthusiastic financial manager in her thirties.

Our financial department had always been run efficiently. Even though we were frequently very tight for money, we always knew what our current financial situation was – and what it might look like in a few months' time. We did monthly and annual budgets, and produced regular cash flows. Each invoice that came into the building was approved by the person who was responsible for it, then passed to the financial manager to organize payment. Before any money left the building, I would review every payment so that I had a sense of how our money was being spent. Our warehouse invoices were reviewed in detail by Philip. This regular discipline made us very aware of all our costs.

When I was young I had moved primary school at the age of nine and skipped a year of classes. As a result, I never really made up for the lost year and struggled with maths. Luckily, I have plenty of common sense and if there were difficult calculations to be done I would ask the accounts department to help. I always wanted to know the overdraft balance every morning and how much cash was in the bank; and I could sense how well we were doing when I reviewed that together with the cash flow. We were still receiving the bulk of our turnover on an agreed date from the warehouse, so we were able to plan ahead as best we could. But there was never enough cash to clear the overdraft, which had gradually grown higher every year that we had been in business. Luckily, the value of our building in Windmill Street had too, which was why we were able to continue increasing our borrowings.

Our management consultants recommended a freelance financial consultant to us to help us look at the figures from a different viewpoint. He would come into the office on a regular basis to check we weren't doing anything that would lead us towards disaster. We liked working with him; Preeya and I found him a good person to talk to. He helped us to schedule and plan, and think about how our decisions might have implications regarding tax or other financial repercussions.

The months went by, and our new team was becoming very powerful in a short time. We all felt more energized when we came into the office in the mornings, and this new confidence affected everyone in the building. We were going places again.

TWENTY EIGHT
NORA

The success of our Zoe Barnes chick lit novels led to our being offered more talented authors for our fiction list. By now, too, we had become more experienced at packaging our books so that they looked every bit as good as any other paperback house's titles. One day, I received a call from the London agent who represented Nora Roberts. At that time, Nora was probably the most successful author of women's commercial fiction in the world, and she continues to be up there with the best. Highly prolific, each novel she writes becomes a new American bestseller. The agent, feeling that Nora wasn't as well known in the UK as she wanted her to be, was looking for a new home for her. She had seen how we had managed to build Zoe's profile and sales in the UK and – because she knew we would put Nora at the top of our fiction programme – she wondered whether we could achieve the same with her.

I was immediately thrilled with the idea of publishing Nora. She writes psychological thrillers with wonderful, memorable characters and is also a brilliant romance writer. We had published one of her novels ten years earlier for the library market, so I was already familiar with her work. Now, we tentatively dipped a toe in the water, starting with her psychological thrillers. We created a new cover style for the first book, *Home Port*, which showed scenery rather than a woman's face. The next novel came only six months later, and then a third. All good so far, but then there was a catch: the agent wanted us to take on all of Nora's new work. Under the pseudonym J. D. Robb, she had recently developed a completely new series of thrillers that were set in the future. They had already been published in the UK and hadn't made much impact, and it was an ongoing, long series. We said we would dedicate ourselves to building it, alongside our other new Nora titles.

Nora was used to writing several books a year, and for our programme there would be one psychological thriller each year, a trilogy of romances which would be published straight into paperback over an eighteen-month period, and one or sometimes two new J. D. Robb novels. There would be lots of wonderful material to work with, but it was also going to require huge planning on our part in order to schedule the books in such a way that we would be able to maximize the potential of each individual title and avoid the accusation of overpublishing. Working closely with Gillian, our new fiction director, we came up with the idea of using a powerful single photographic image on each cover for the J. D. Robb series. The first cover images included a butterfly, a white lily, a red rose, and a pink candle, and these were followed by others such as a cobweb, a snowflake, forks of lightning, and other varieties of flowers. The images were designed in such a way as to look both stark and soft at the same time, and the series looked very powerful when placed on the bookshelf in a row, face or spine out.

Reprinting recently published novels by a little-known author is always a risk. We hoped the strikingly designed J. D. Robb covers would differentiate the books in the series sufficiently from all the other Nora Roberts novels; and we used the banner head "Nora Roberts writing as J. D. Robb" to help give the series more traction. Luckily the strategy worked, and booksellers were happy to order stock of "both" authors.

We invested heavily in building Nora's sales not only in the UK but in our largest export markets – Australia, New Zealand and South Africa – where we were allowed to sell her books exclusively. Our new packaging for all the books worked well and Nora's sales began to increase everywhere. The print runs grew longer – more money out, but more money coming in – and I had no choice but to borrow more money to pay for the increased advances and all the print and marketing costs. The company turnover and the overdraft were increasing in tandem.

After we had been publishing Nora for a couple of years, we sounded out the agent as to whether Nora would be interested in coming to the UK. Fortunately she was; Nora has very strong Irish roots – many of her books have an Irish setting – and she always loves to visit Ireland. She agreed to come to London for one day and then she and I would both travel to Ireland, where she would do a further day's publicity in Dublin.

Inviting the world's most famous author to visit was a massive undertaking for us. I had sleepless nights for several days before the trip and I remember that when I met Nora on the steps of her hotel in Langham Place, I nearly didn't recognize her, even though I had been staring at her photo on book covers for months. I have always struggled to remember people's faces – it's a condition called prosopagnosia, face blindness, and it has got me into trouble on many occasions.

Jana had arranged several media interviews; radio was the first, and we later returned to the hotel where Nora gave interviews in her suite. Nora was pleasant and charming – she must have met so many publishers and publicity people in her many years as a successful writer and she was a complete professional, making it very easy for us to work with her. Diane had been able to organize a small and exclusive dinner for key book buyers for that first evening. At the time, the famous chef Gordon Ramsay had a restaurant franchise in Claridge's hotel and there was a private room off the dining area which we hired for the evening. The food was amazing and the chef himself came in to greet us and to check that everything was OK. I had read all of Nora's novels that we had published – probably ten or twelve by then – and she and I spent a wonderful evening discussing and comparing many of the characters from her books. It was as if they were all people we both knew.

The next day, we visited Dublin where there were more media interviews and a book signing in the largest central bookstore. The queue stretched out the door. Nora's Irish fans are legion and she made time to speak to as many as she could.

I loved my visit to Dublin. After Nora left, I stayed on for an extra two days and Leah, my younger daughter, flew over to accompany me. Together, we feasted on all the gorgeous Irish bookshops, soaking up the atmosphere. Ireland has always been a wonderful market for book lovers and we came home with a suitcase-full. I always enjoy seeing what bookshops in other countries choose to stock on their shelves and can rarely manage to walk out of a bookshop anywhere in the world without buying something that I probably wouldn't find easily at home.

Everything had gone well on Nora's promotional trip. She had behaved with great generosity towards us, appreciating that we didn't have the same budgets as her huge American publishers, and we could not have been more grateful. It felt like a true partnership. The results of such a trip can't be quantified immediately, but, as the months and years progressed, sales of Nora's books in all our markets continued to increase. We kept breaking new records for ourselves and for Nora. Her new Piatkus-published novels gradually went to the top of the bestseller lists in all our export markets, Australia, New Zealand and South Africa. Shortly after Nora became a number one bestseller in South Africa, a bouquet of flowers arrived one day. The card said simply, "From Nora."

Philip was responsible for all our export sales and over the years had always visited Australia at least once a year, as that was our biggest market – along with New Zealand, South Africa and the Far East. Every few years, I would travel to all those countries as well, to meet customers and our sales colleagues and to get a feel for their marketplace. I loved these foreign trips and always tried to stay on for a holiday if at all possible. Australia has always had a special place in my heart.

One year, I was in New Zealand and seeing a key buyer for one of the major book wholesalers, pitching Nora as best I could. I told her that whenever Nora wrote a new romantic trilogy, the books were published straight into paperback and immediately went to the top of the American bestseller list, each one frequently selling in excess of two million copies. "Two million copies!" exclaimed the young buyer. "Two million women can't be wrong. I'll definitely be ordering a lot for our shops." And of course two million women couldn't be wrong. But it was much harder to persuade our British buyers of that. When we first began to work to build Nora's profile, we would get all manner of complaints – even though Nora's books sold in every country of the world and had been translated into so many languages. "I think she should change her name," said one English male buyer. "Nora sounds so old-fashioned." It really was hard work some days.

For several years I would wake up thinking, "How can we sell more of Nora's books today?" Because there were always so many of them coming through, we were always looking for new ways to promote her. We advertised on the tube and in women's magazines and we gave away hundreds of free copies so that readers could try one for themselves. At one point, we supplied twenty thousand J. D. Robb books to the London *Evening Standard* to give to commuters. Thinking of new ways to expand her market was a constant challenge, but we were always up for it. Nora's sales were climbing and so was our turnover and our profits. I would negotiate with her agent to buy five books at a time and, as her sales increased, we would offer higher advances. I had to find a figure that recognized the growth of our sales and which was, at the same time, affordable. It was a very delicate balancing act, and we had to be vigilant about how much of our growing success was dependent on just one author. We always had a Plan B in our minds in case she was attracted away by another company. Were that to happen, even with her backlist, which was growing at the rate of five or six new books a year for us, our turnover would probably drop by £1,000,000 to £2,000,000 within a twelve- to eighteen-month period. It was a sobering thought and one we constantly kept in the back of our minds. Although we were so excited by our success with Nora's books, we never took our good fortune for granted.

TWENTY NINE
PORTRAIT

By now, Piatkus had become part of the British publishing establishment and we proudly put together a substantial catalogue, promoting our backlist titles as we approached our twenty-first birthday. On 22 March 2001, a memorable day for the British book trade took place: Her Majesty the Queen held a reception for "the great and the good" of the British publishing industry at Buckingham Palace. We knew the company had arrived when I received an invitation.

It was an amazing experience to be driven in a taxi down the Mall, through the huge, tall gates into the inner court and then ascend the stairs into the palace itself. The gathering consisted of famous authors such as J. K. Rowling and Ian Rankin, well-known heads of publishing companies and industry trade bodies, literary agents and booksellers. Many of us knew each other and were chattering amongst ourselves when there was a sudden hush. I turned to see the Queen standing a few feet away from me. Although small in stature, her aura was so powerful that the room gradually fell silent.

At one point in the evening, an equerry approached me and asked if I would like to meet the Queen. Standing in line, I waited for my turn. When it came, she asked me what I did and I wished I had been able to tell her that I published books about dogs or horses as I am sure she would have found that more interesting than my telling her that I ran an independent publishing company. Next to me in the line was a bookseller from Scotland who told the Queen that, as young girls, she and her sister remembered watching the Queen through their window as she visited Glasgow just after the war. The Queen smiled warmly at her and said, "Yes, I remember that visit as well. It was a very special time."

That visit to Buckingham Palace was followed a couple of years later by one to Downing Street when we published *Survival in the City* by Mrs Moneypenny, who had a popular column in the *Financial Times*. Heather McGregor (the author's real name) was donating some of the proceeds from the book to a charity run by Sarah Brown, wife of the Chancellor of the Exchequer at the time, Gordon Brown, who subsequently became Prime Minister. I was introduced to him and he made a lively and entertaining speech. There's a picture of all of us standing outside Number 10 afterwards, which hangs above my desk next to my college certificates. It was an incredible evening.

There's one other framed photograph, of a yellowing press cutting, on the wall next to it. I was shopping one Saturday morning when I got a frantic call on my mobile from my cousin. "I've just seen that article about you and Prince Charles in *The Times* this morning," she said. "Congratulations." Having never met the Prince, I had absolutely no idea what she was talking about and, intrigued, I rushed off to buy a copy.

The features section that day had published a piece, "The 50 Movers and Shakers Who Define How Well We Live", and there, in a little section within the article entitled "The Alternative Thinkers", were photographs of Prince Charles and Anita Roddick of the Body Shop with one of me between them. At the base of the article, a strapline read: "A nation of uptight Brits suddenly started sharing their issues." It seemed so pertinent, after my own therapy and counselling experiences in which I'd had to share my own issues, that I couldn't help but laugh.

In spite of these new accolades, I still felt we were never taken as seriously as many other publishers in the UK because of the areas in which we published and for which our brand was well known. Our fiction list was going from strength to strength, with the success of Nora's titles encouraging agents and American publishers to offer us strong new authors, but our non-fiction needed a boost. Over the years we had published books by many interesting non-fiction authors, including Arianna Huffington's autobiography *The Fourth Instinct*, Arlie Hochschild's seminal work *The Second Shift* and a vast range of other general non-fiction, including history, military and gift book titles and assorted biographies of such eminent people as Tiger Woods, Wasim Akram, Rupert Murdoch and Quentin Tarantino. Nevertheless, our general non-fiction list had never quite come together in one cohesive whole. The business, mind, body, spirit (MBS) and psychology shelves were always hidden away in the bookshops, and we wanted to see more of our books on the front-of-store display tables. The team decided, as a result, that we would launch a new brand that would showcase general non-fiction books, those which might have a chance of being displayed prominently. We held a competition within the office for people to think up names for this new imprint. Several members of staff contributed good ideas but none felt quite right.

Cyril and I took a long-weekend break in Hereford that autumn. We were wandering round the cathedral, admiring the showcases of exquisite items, when the name for the imprint suddenly came to me. *Portrait*, I thought. *Let's call it Portrait.* We ran with the name – the "P" alliteration worked well – and devised a new logo for Portrait, using one of the little circles from our Piatkus four-leaf clover-type design. We wanted to publish history, biography, sport, military, gift and popular culture under the new brand and our non-fiction team set about looking for suitable books for it.

Portrait launched in 2003 and we had fun with it. Some of our notable successes were very different from our previous books: we published the autobiography of rugby legend Willie John McBride; a quirky gift book entitled *The Strange Laws of Old England*, which sold very well at Christmas; and a biography of Julie Andrews, ordered in large quantities by the supermarkets, which became our first Portrait bestseller. Several were published first in hardback, and the higher cover prices were always welcome.

Another area of the market that we began to explore in 2005 was that of the environment and climate change. As usual, we were largely ahead of the game. The early signs of the present climate crisis were all there in the first decade of this century, but the public were not yet ready to listen. Our books, such as that of Professor Ervin Laszlo – which discussed how the world had reached a tipping point – were well reviewed in the media but that didn't translate into sales. Now the topic is on everyone's minds and we all know that each of us has a responsibility to do what we can to make a difference.

Two Piatkus books that did do extremely well for us around that time contributed hugely to our backlist. *Getting Things Done* by David Allen, written in response to the problem of the growing email in-box, became one of our top-selling titles of all time. Selling around 2,000 copies a month, it was a reminder that we could still get it right in the business book area. The other title, one we came up with after discussing current trends, was Fiona Fullerton's *How to Make Money from Your Property*. At the time, she had a weekly column at the back of the *Sunday Times* magazine where she wrote about her experiences as a landlady. We paid the author one of our highest advances ever (which, happily, was to earn out so that we eventually paid the author royalties as well), but we thought it was worth the risk as everyone was discussing the property boom.

Some days, during those final years, it felt like there was a lot to be thankful for. We always celebrated everything we could – cakes for birthdays and company successes and regular drinks and lunches for special occasions and leaving dos. We had an annual staff day out, which took us to Paris, Brussels and Lille in various years. Every Christmas, we would hold a party for our authors in the attractive Curwen & New Academy art gallery across the road from the office in Windmill Street. We figured that most of our authors must always be hearing about publishing parties but would have rarely been invited to them, and here they could meet the staff who'd worked on their books. It was also an opportunity for our freelancers to socialize with our staff and to meet the authors whose books they had worked on.

Although we had many successes to celebrate, we also had our fair share of frustrating misses. Following our success with Nora Roberts, over a couple of years we'd become the publishers of many of the best commercial women authors on the American bestseller lists. Other British publishers had not been interested in taking them on, so we had been able to buy their latest books and their backlists very cheaply. Susan Elizabeth Phillips, Linda Howard, Jayne Anne Krentz, Stephanie Laurens, Julia Quinn, Gaelen Foley and Mary Balogh were all hugely popular as online bestsellers for us; and we then expanded our range even further with popular paranormal romance writers Christine Feehan, Sherrilyn Kenyon, Keri Arthur, J. R. Ward and MaryJanice Davidson, who were also much loved. It was hard not to feel gutted when we missed out on some authors, though; we couldn't always get it right. Suzanne Collins, whose work we were offered and turned down, wrote *The Hunger Games* trilogy – titles we hadn't been entirely convinced we could sell in our market. It is always very hard to spot which authors will be the most successful. Publishing is always such a personal business and there are so many books at any one time that you are offered. The trick is to try to get it right some of the time at least. That is all any publisher can do.

Quietly, and unnoticed by most of our competitors, we gradually built up a new range of paperback fiction by these wonderful authors, whose new titles soon turned into a fast-growing fiction backlist. I particularly liked Susan Elizabeth Phillips, who wrote witty romantic comedies, and Mary Balogh, whose novels were set in Regency England and had very feisty heroines. When I went to America or Australia I would see the shelves of these novelists' books – many of whom were hugely successful in their own countries as well as in the UK and abroad – in the supermarkets and bookshops, and it was so exciting to count how many of them were being published on the Piatkus list, knowing we were successfully building them in our market.

Another opportunity came our way during the period of our five-year plan. Reid Tracy, CEO of the American publishing company Hay House, called us one day to gauge our interest in distributing their books in the UK market. We had long admired our colleagues there and were delighted to have the opportunity to sell their mind, body, spirit books alongside our own. We were visiting so many specialist outlets, it made complete sense. Both Diane and Philip always liked having a new challenge and very much enjoyed working with the Hay House team to help build their sales and reputation in the UK market.

Over the next few years, the turnover grew by £1,000,000 a year and the profit ratio climbed too. When we had a good year we paid additional bonuses to key staff members. We had always paid a week's Christmas bonus in good years. In the past, whenever we'd had a difficult trading season everyone in the office always knew – you could feel it in the air – but, now, people were feeling very proud of all our achievements. Everyone knew that what they were working on made a difference to the overall purpose and success of the company. And so it was that with amazing teamwork and much dedicated creativity, together with luck and good timing, four years after our fateful meeting with the turnaround team, our turnover had virtually doubled, our profits had gone up tremendously and suddenly we were in sight of our £10,000,000 goal.

THIRTY
EXIT

I had always known, in the back of my mind, that one day I would want to sell the company. I loved it and everything that all of us who worked there had achieved together. It felt as if my little boat, sailing on the ocean in stormy seas in the early years, had grown into a fully-fledged galleon. The seas were still stormy, but now we had more ballast to withstand the gales. (At the same time, we might not survive a hurricane: no business can ever be 100 percent weatherproof.)

In the early years of the company I had promised my two co-directors, Gill and Philip, that they would receive a percentage of the proceeds should the company be sold one day. They had trusted me with the best years of their careers. The company had done well with the combined efforts of the three of us overseeing the business. Now it was up to me to make good on my promise.

My younger children were of college age and neither of them had expressed an interest in coming into the company. Not everyone is cut out to be an entrepreneur and join the family business, even if they have commercial instincts, and I had always wanted them to follow their hearts, above all, and find the career path that was right for them. I had been so fortunate in being able to do what I loved and I hoped they would be able to find the same rewards and satisfaction when they made their own life choices.

Philip, Gill and I had proven our trust for each other many times over; now it was time to turn our agreed terms – made twenty-five years ago with a handshake – into a legal contract. Each of us had to employ our own set of lawyers to draw up the agreement. It was a horribly fraught time: we had worked together for more than twenty years and always got on brilliantly, but now each of us had to avoid our professional teams becoming adversarial. No one wanted to fall out over it. Eventually, however, we were able to navigate the rapids and everything was signed.

We had achieved all our goals after four years. It had been an incredible time. Only the three of us had known that my likely aim at the end of our five-year plan would be to sell the company. I'd wanted to go out on a high and had understood that the company would be of far more value if potential buyers could see a clear growth trajectory continuing after my personal exit. Because of the growing success of Nora Roberts's books in our territories and the flourishing new fiction backlist, the turnover had climbed at a very fast rate and, as a result, we had become more profitable. The first decade of the twentieth-first century was a good period to grow a business; the financial markets were booming and there was plenty of money around. Now, too, because of the internet, it wasn't necessary to go to America to find out what the new trends were; I could sit at home, log on to my computer and research expert opinions from all over the world.

As I researched these trends, it was steadily becoming clear to me that two major ones would impact on the book trade. The first concerned the future of the book. Amazon was developing its Kindle and other companies were following suit. We had hundreds of contracts with American publishers, and it was hard to guess how the market would agree to divide up the income from books that were sold on handheld readers. We owned the right to print our books and sell them in our market, but would that still be the case in a few years' time, when publishers would be publishing both printed editions and e-books? (As it happened, American publishers did continue to divide up proceeds according to traditional terms, but it was not obvious at the early stages of e-books that this would happen.)

Secondly, and more importantly, I was increasingly coming across commentators in the financial world who were expressing the view that the financial bubble would burst before too long and there would be a global recession. I didn't know if they were right, but I did know to be wary of recessions. Piatkus Books had survived a few downturns. Many of the books we were publishing sold well during recessions – escapist fiction, health and business books, and spiritual books – but, nevertheless, recession means less money around for everyone and often a time when one's best customers don't always survive.

There was also another cloud on the horizon. We had done incredibly well with our sales of Nora Roberts's novels and had got her to number one on the bestseller lists in Australia, New Zealand and South Africa, our major export markets. We had, after a lot of work, achieved supermarket sales for her in the UK and her new novels were now being displayed on all the new-title tables in the bookshops. Her new J. D. Robb hardbacks were getting into the bestseller lists, but we hadn't yet achieved bestseller status in the UK for the author's titles under her own name. Because of that, there was a distinct possibility that Nora and her American agent might decide that she should move to a larger company. They had always been very loyal and supportive, but this wasn't about loyalty; Nora's agent – who I got on very well with – might feel that she wasn't doing the best for Nora if she didn't give her the opportunity to move to a larger company. And if Nora were to move to another publishing house, the value of our company would drop significantly overnight. Piatkus Books would survive – we had future contracts for a few as yet unwritten and unpublished books which would help to tide us over the first couple of years before we had to manage without her – but Nora was the jewel in our crown and future purchasers would take that into consideration when they valued the company.

We reflected carefully on the future. We were all growing older and so were several members of our important and very valued team. We'd had a great time working together and had built a successful enterprise with which we were all very proud to be associated. Did we have the necessary energy to reinvent it again – partly for the leaner times ahead and partly for the forthcoming technological age? We came to the conclusion that we should quit while we were ahead. Now that the paperwork for the transfer of shares had been dealt with, I turned my mind to the preparations for the sale.

I had long ago decided that, if I ever were to sell the company, I would like to work with Kit van Tulleken of the Van Tulleken agency. Her organization was, in my opinion, the best company to handle the sale. It did not occur to me for one moment that I would not invite an intermediary to handle the sale: I did not consider that negotiation was my strong point and I thought I would soon have been out of my depth. I also understood that it might get emotional and that I would need someone objective to stand in my corner with me. It was time to let the professionals who were expert in buying and selling companies take over.

During the time Piatkus Books had been in existence, we had published over 3,000 original books. Some authors had asked for their rights back when their books went out of print, but, for the most part, we had a printed contract for each title, along with many contracts for sales of foreign licences. In one of our board meetings, I put forward the suggestion that we should digitize all these in case of fire or flood, so we arranged for someone to come in and do the work, an onerous task that took several weeks. At the same time, we digitized all our key documents and contracts for the office. We drew up budgets for the year ahead in the normal way and continued to commission and purchase good books. Everything, seemingly, was carrying on as normal, but we were getting our house in order ready for the sale.

I felt that the fewer people who knew about the planned sale the better; it seemed to me that our staff would find it less unsettling that way. We had all worked so closely as a team and the trust between us all ran deep. It seemed to me that this was the right thing to do, causing less anxiety to everyone. The truth was that we might not achieve our aim and, if that were to happen, we would have spared them weeks of unnecessary worry. For twenty-seven years I'd had an open door policy – anyone in the company could come into my office and have a conversation with me at any time I was free. Now I was needing to close the door for parts of the day when I was expecting cryptic phone calls, and I hated it. Having to hold such an enormous secret, one which would cause a lot of unhappiness, caused me untold stress, especially as I had always prided myself on my openness.

The weeks went by. Preeya produced her regular future budgets and sets of figures, all of which I shared with the Van Tulleken company who were working to put a substantial proposal together. Finally, the call came to say that all the paperwork for the proposal had been assembled and we were ready to go. The day had come when I had to pick up the phone to Nora's agent in America. The London Book Fair was coming up and she would be travelling to London for it. We had a somewhat cryptic conversation where I asked her not to think about moving Nora to another publisher before she had talked to me. She got the message. Gradually we were putting everything in place so that nothing would stand in the way of an easy, well-managed sale.

Because we now had so many commercial novelists in our publishing programme, we knew we needed a purchaser who would know how to maximize the potential of all our wonderful books in mass-market paperback. This narrowed the list of potential purchasers, which was good because we didn't want to offer the company too widely. We also needed to sell to a company with whom Nora's agent would be happy to deal. Everyone who received the sales proposal would be able to understand why they had been offered our beautiful company.

The other issue that was important to me – so much so that we put it in the proposal – was that I wanted to sell to a corporation who would retain most, if not all, of the staff. If our employees were to choose to move on, that was up to them, but I was concerned that as many people as possible should continue to receive their salary at the end of each month while they decided what they would like their new future to look like.

The clock was ticking. Van Tulleken had set a date for offers to be received. I felt like I was living a double life, and it was horrible. Having to behave as if everything was normal, I would sit in meetings talking about our plans for our forthcoming books, while also discussing and commissioning interesting books that I knew I might never be around to see published. Everything in the office was carrying on as normal but my mind was in another space all together. It wasn't at all comfortable but I didn't feel that I had a choice, believing as I did that my actions were in the best interests of everyone concerned.

Eventually the responses to the sale document began to arrive. We received three offers for the company, one of which – from Tim Hely Hutchinson and Ursula Mackenzie of Hachette – was head and shoulders above the rest. At the time the largest general publishing company in the UK (owned by the Lagardère Group in France), Hachette's offer was very simple. It would acquire Piatkus, which would be managed under its Little, Brown imprint, of which Ursula was the managing director. We had not offered the building in Windmill Street in the sale; in any event, they did not want it. Their whole group was about to move into a new building near Blackfriars Bridge and they wanted Piatkus Books to join them there at the beginning of November, just a few months away. The only condition they made was that I stay on for a further six months after the contract was signed to be available, when needed, for the period of the handover. When Van Tulleken had sent out the proposal, they had made it clear to the potential purchasers that it was a retirement sale. I was not prepared to start working for another boss at this point in my life. After all, I hadn't worked for anyone since I was twenty-four.

My two co-directors and I felt the Hachette offer was exactly what we had hoped for. The Little, Brown group of imprints would be a good fit, as none of their brands was similar to ours. Little, Brown had a very strong record of successful paperback publishing and would know the best way to sell our books. They were also offering to keep on nearly all our staff. Only four out of twenty-eight would have to look for a new job, and there might be a role for them in another of the Hachette companies. It was the end of June 2007 when the offer came through. We accepted it immediately.

With a company as old as ours due diligence could take several months. It was frustrating as we were all in a hurry. Now I had a prospective buyer, I wanted to move as quickly as possible to complete the sale. The secrecy was killing me. The holiday season would soon be upon us and Hachette's office move wasn't far off. It was in everyone's interests to get the due diligence done as quickly as possible. At this point, I took Preeya and Simon into my confidence. Their jobs would continue at Little, Brown and, for the moment, Simon would be needed to oversee production of all the forthcoming titles that we were continuing to acquire, while Preeya needed to make available all our accounting procedures to the Little, Brown team and to oversee the financial housekeeping. Piatkus had always been up to date with our housekeeping. I was so lucky to have Preeya and Simon working with me as both were extremely well organized. Their record-keeping was exemplary; there would be few queries that couldn't be quickly sorted out.

At the time of the sale, the company had an overdraft of £1,000,000 resting on my slim shoulders and we also had other borrowings. The building had been our security against these loans, which had to be cleared. The company had been banking with the same high street branch in the suburbs since the early

1980s, our account now managed by the corporate department. Over the years, I had worked with thirteen different bank managers, some good, some not so good, and one who was particularly dire. Few of them had actually understood how our business worked but our results were consistent; we had a good track record of nearly always making a profit, even though it was often very small. The present bank manager was very affable. When I rang to tell him we had sold the company, he sounded shocked when I revealed how much it was worth; maybe he had little experience of intellectual property in the publishing world. I even fantasised that he might have bought me lunch after one of our annual meetings to renew the overdraft if he had known.

I rang the turnaround team as well to thank them for helping us to get on the right road. They were surprised but very happy for us, telling me that while they had liked the five-year plan we had to put together, they hadn't actually expected that we would succeed in achieving our goal. Perhaps they too hadn't fully understood the value of our intellectual property.

Thanks to Preeya, the due diligence was finished very efficiently within four weeks, an extraordinary achievement for a company with twenty-eight years of intellectual property and thousands of contracts and financial records. A date was agreed for the signature of the sale documents, a Friday towards the end of July 2007. It was raining hard in London that morning. The Hachette and Little, Brown people, together with the Van Tulleken team and our Piatkus lawyers, assembled in the City office of the Hachette lawyers. Many different documents kept being placed in front of myself and Gill and Philip. We decided to trust our lawyers, and initialled and signed page after page; there certainly wasn't enough time to read everything through. When, finally, the deed was done, bottles of champagne were opened and wheeled into the room on a dainty gold trolley. We sat at the long boardroom table, sipping slowly. I thanked Little, Brown for being so easy to work with and made a toast, saying that I hoped the company would do even better for them than they had hoped and expected, and that they would never regret their purchase of our beautiful gem.

Tim told us a transfer of monies was being made to the accounts of all the shareholders that afternoon. The money probably wouldn't arrive that day, as it was after twelve noon, but it would be there for Monday. The champagne was cleared. The lawyers charging by the hour removed themselves to earn more money. Gill had another appointment to go to, so Philip and I left and found a local Starbucks where we perched on high stools staring out at the busy City street. For once, neither of us had much to say. For me, the whole day leading up to that moment had felt completely surreal.

After an hour or so, we separated. It was still pouring with rain as I caught the train back to Edgware, where that morning – it seemed an age ago already – I had left my much-loved but shabby fifteen-year-old Volvo in the station car park. We had some friends coming round for drinks at the weekend, although I knew I wouldn't be ready to talk about what had just happened. I went into the Marks and Spencer food hall by the tube station and stood deliberating in front of a shelf of olives. There was a particular kind I liked but didn't always buy as they were rather expensive. As I stood there wondering if I should treat myself, I suddenly realized that, on this day of all days, I could buy all the jars on the whole shelf if I wanted to.

Less than two months later, Northern Rock, a high street building society based in the North East of England, became the victim of the first run on a UK bank for over a century: people stood in large queues outside branches of the bank throughout the country, all trying to withdraw their money at the same time. Would the value of Piatkus Books have gone down after that? Almost certainly. The Northern Rock collapse was the first sign of the global recession that was to follow. In business, timing is everything, and you never have any control over that.

THIRTY ONE

END TIMES

It was the last week of October 2007 and our final day in the office at 5 Windmill Street. For several weeks now, all the staff had been busy decluttering, sorting files and packing boxes in preparation for the move to join Little, Brown in their new offices by Blackfriars Station, on the edge of London's City district. Our new Little, Brown colleagues were moving in just a few days before us.

Little, Brown's team of staff had been extraordinarily efficient. While we at Piatkus sat around in the office for several weeks, many of us still in a state of shock and disbelief, they had quietly come in and begun to remove all the paperwork they needed in order to take the company forward. They had planned out the new staffing structure for all the departments and decided where everyone would sit in the new building. All their staff would, like ours, soon be experiencing a new open-plan style of workplace. People would be perched at long desks in rows, with four seats facing four others and with only a few feet of desk space separating one person from another. Everyone already understood the advantages of working closely with colleagues and the financial benefit to the company of an open-plan office, but it was still going to take some getting used to after the spacious area the Piatkus team were leaving behind.

So much had happened so quickly. I thought back to that Monday morning when I had come into Windmill Street after

I had finalized the sale of the company. Little, Brown had prepared a press release announcing the sale, which would go out to the book trade at eleven o'clock that morning.

At ten o'clock, I called all the Piatkus staff together for a meeting on the first floor. My heart was in my mouth as I broke the news that the company had been sold on the Friday of the previous week. I hadn't prepared a speech because I wanted the words to come spontaneously. In the end, I told them, "I have been working at Piatkus every day of my life for the past twenty-eight years. That's longer than some of you have been alive. I am sorry but I just can't do it anymore." I could hear my voice breaking as I said the last sentence. I knew it was true. I had used up all my strength in the years that had gone by. Aside from my venture into counselling, I had rarely taken any time away from the office other than my regular annual vacation. The concept of a sabbatical was rare in the commercial world. I had never had the chance to rest from the business. It really was time to put down all the responsibility I had been carrying.

I told my colleagues about the new company, explained what a good opportunity I truly felt it was for the business that carried my name, and thanked them for being so amazing and for everything that they had done. Some people were crying. The atmosphere was tense and sad. Everyone returned to their desks to absorb the news.

Little, Brown had hired the first floor of L'Etoile, the restaurant round the corner in Charlotte Street where my old boss David Higham used to lunch each day. They had invited everyone for a drink that afternoon to give them a chance to meet a few of their new colleagues. Naturally, people were subdued and they were relieved to hear Little, Brown confirm that very few jobs would be lost.

By the time I sold the company, several of my close colleagues had been working with me and each other for upwards of twenty years. Nearly everyone else in the company had been there for more than three years. We had been such a close-knit team, with only twenty-eight people on the payroll. We had all known and understood each other so well. We had supported each other's strengths and found ways to work around each other's weaknesses. We had cheered each other on when times were bad and celebrated during the good times. Together, we had formed an amazing group, punching far above our weight. Our bonds ran very deep after all these years spent working in harmony together. I knew I would miss them all so much.

After the sale, the question I was asked most frequently was about my plans for the future. I would then explain that one of the conditions of the company sale was that I had to sign a non-compete clause, which meant I couldn't set up another publishing company for three years. I didn't mind about that. I was, at least for the time being, quite sure I wouldn't be launching another company any time in the near future. I was looking forward to some downtime instead.

Many people struggled with the idea of my not having a future plan. "But you have always worked so hard," they said. "We can't imagine you doing nothing."

"Well, I'm going to do nothing," I told the enquirers. "I shall sit around in coffee shops, having deep conversations with interesting people. I will love having the time to do that. It's my favourite activity."

Now here I was, sitting at my desk in Windmill Street for the very last time. I had decided to sell the building and the estate agents were coming round to value it for me early the next week. I had been so happy here, but it held too many precious memories. I wanted a clean break from all of it. I had read lots of poignant novels that described important moments in characters' lives. As I sat at my desk I thought I ought to be feeling something very profound. I was aware that in future months when I felt down, as I was sure I sometimes would, I would think back to this moment and recall what it was like. I searched for words to describe how I felt. At first the only feeling I had was of numbness. But then I began to think about how extraordinarily grateful I was.

I believe that each one of us comes into the world with unique talents and gifts, but not all of us have the opportunity to use them in the way we would ideally choose. My unique gifts were a flair for entrepreneurship and for publishing, and during this long period of my working life I had had the great good fortune to be able to combine the two. I had been privileged to open readers' minds to new ways of thinking – as well as to inspire, inform and entertain them.

An ability to get along with most people had enabled my colleagues and myself to create a workspace where each of us could bring out the best in one another. I could not have done any of this of my own volition; everything had been about teamwork. But as a leader, there were so many times when I had instinctively known what we needed to do. My gut instincts, intuition and experience had helped to find solutions to problems whenever we needed them.

I knew I had been very lucky to enjoy a fulfilling career. Many people want to run their own businesses but not everyone is gifted with the right mindset. My generally even and practical temperament had enabled me to take problems in my stride. I trusted my instincts and I was not afraid of hard work. When invited to give talks about what qualities are needed for successful entrepreneurial ventures, during a time when capital was easier to come by, I would often say, "Persistence and hard work, focus, teamwork and, of course, timing."

I had had a beautiful life in publishing. I had touched the depths and scaled the heights. Ever since I had been a young woman, I had been able to spend my time engaged in, what was for me, meaningful and purposeful work. There had been a wonderful beginning, an amazing middle period and now a triumphant ending to all of it.

So, what would I do next? I sighed. I had no plans, but I would soon find out. I knew that, for me too, tomorrow would also be another day.

EPILOGUE

A little more than a year after selling the company, I happened to wander into a branch of the independent bookseller Daunt Books. It had been a fraught week. The global financial crisis was making headlines on every news bulletin and a number of banks in Iceland had gone bankrupt. The then Prime Minister, Gordon Brown, was still deliberating about whether to bail out the English banks and support the hundreds of thousands of people who would lose all their savings if the British branches of the Icelandic banks collapsed.

As I paused by the shop till, there right in front of me was a book entitled *The Great Crash* by Selwyn Parker. Piatkus had commissioned it in the spring of 2007, right before I sold the company. Now it was being published in the exact same week as the greatest financial crisis that most people had ever experienced.

Standing there, I felt such a high, such a sense of the emotional rewards at the end of my career. Even though I no longer owned the company and would earn not a penny from it ever again, the astute timing of the publication of that book felt like the perfect swansong. Right up until the very last minute of our independent existence, we had got it right.

ACKNOWLEDGEMENTS

Gill, Philip, Diane, Jana, Simon, Preeya, Gillian – thank you for being the most wonderful travelling companions during our journey with Piatkus Books. Thank you also for reading this book at an early stage and for your helpful comments – even the unexpected ones.

To everyone who was employed by Piatkus Books during the twenty-eight years of its independent existence, a massive thank you for making the company such a positive experience for so many who worked there. I wish I could have included and acknowledged more of you in these pages. I hope this book will remind you of many good experiences and friendships.

To all the people who worked alongside our team at Piatkus – our fabulous freelance colleagues, all the printers, both large and small, agents of every kind, both at home and abroad, and everyone who supported our independent company over the years – thank you for believing in us and for championing and supporting us.

To all the wonderful, amazing and talented authors who came to Piatkus with your work – thank you for allowing us to be your publishers and for contributing so much pleasure to all your readers.

To Etan, Fiona, Laura, Vicky, Rachel, Fizza, Daniel and my new colleagues at independent publisher Watkins – it has been a wonderful experience to work with you all and I am so grateful for your enthusiasm and for everything that you have done to make this book a success.

To Wanda, for your generous encouragement, unstinting support and beautiful command of words.

To Sue, for asking all the right questions and for such thoughtful editing.

To all the lovely people who were kind enough to read and comment on the book at any early stage, thank you for your time – especially Kathy, Lucy, Kate, Tess and Liz.

To Jane and colleagues at Graham Maw Christie – thank you for all your hard work and your patience and persistence.

To Laura and Gavin of BookMachine, a special thank you for being always ready to listen, help and advise.

To Matthew and Sonia, Jonny, Hannah, Sylvie and Jamie – always in my heart and in my thoughts.

Finally, of course no words would ever be enough to say thank you for the constant love, support and encouragement of Cyril and Leah. Gratitude and blessings in abundance.